Getting into
The Story
of Concord

A HISTORY
OF THE *BOOK OF CONCORD*

David P. Scaer

Publishing House
St. Louis

Unless otherwise stated, the Scripture quotations in this publication are from the Revised Standard Version of the Bible, copyrighted 1946, 1952, © 1971, 1973 by the Division of Christian Education of the National Council of the Churches of Christ in the U.S.A., and used by permission.

Quotations of the Lutheran Confessions are from *The Book of Concord*, tr. and ed. Theodore G. Tappert, © 1959, Fortress Press, Philadelphia, and used by permission.

Concordia Publishing House, St. Louis, Missouri
Copyright © 1977 Concordia Publishing House
MANUFACTURED IN THE UNITED STATES OF AMERICA

Library of Congress Cataloging in Publication Data

Scaer, David P   1936-
    Getting into the story of Concord.

    1. Lutheran Church. Book of Concord. I. Title.
BX8068.S32   238'.4'1   77-13429
ISBN 0-570-03768-9

To
Dorothy
Companion in Life, Faith, and Confession

CONTENTS

I. Honoring a Book

Three years stand out in the history of the Lutheran Reformation: 1517, 1530, and 1580. In 1517 Dr. Martin Luther nailed the Ninety-Five Theses to the door of the Castle Church in Wittenberg, an event still commemorated by Lutherans each Oct. 31. In 1530 certain German Lutheran princes and other civil authorities presented to the emperor of the Holy Roman Empire a document known as the Augsburg Confession. And in 1580 there occurred an event of equal and in some ways greater importance than the other two: the signing and publication of the *Book of Concord*.

The *Book of Concord* is a collection of creeds, books, sermons, and instructional and devotinal essays. These various writings come from different times in a 1,300-year span between A. D. 200 and A.D. 1580. They have been adopted by Lutherans to express to themselves and to others what they believe.

There is an old story about a man who was asked what he believed. He replied that he believed what the church believed. When asked what the church believed, he replied that it believed what he believed. The poor man had argued in a circle, and the questioner remained completely in the dark about what the man and his church believed. Lutherans have a ready-made answer to this kind of dilemma. Even if a member of the Lutheran Church is not absolutely sure about what his church believes, he can direct the questioner to the Lutheran Confessions, which have been collected in the *Book of Concord*.

History remembers men more often than it remembers books and documents. Every nation has holidays honoring its heroes. All Christians honor the birth, death, and resurrection of Jesus Christ, because in these events the church finds her reasons for existing. The various Protestant denominations commemorate the memory of the men who helped formulate their expression of faith. Luther, Zwingli,

Calvin, Knox, and Wesley are all remembered, if not by special holidays, then by buildings, churches, or colleges named in their honor.

Though not as prominent as the memory of men, some documents are treasured and their writing is commemorated. The Magna Carta is that kind of valued document. Very few people have read it, but most of us know in a general way that it guarantees certain rights and privileges, like granting an accused person a trial before a jury of his peers. Like many other documents its ultimate importance was seen only a long time after it had been written. Implications have been drawn from the Magna Carta which could never have been anticipated by its framers. Even though it was written 500 years before our country was established, it set forth principles that became basic to our form of government. The Declaration of Independence, the Constitution, and the Bill of Rights further developed these principles. Rights, obligations, and privileges are assured to the citizens in written documents and do not depend on the whims of government officials. The American Constitution, almost 200 years old, is considered one of the most remarkable documents in political history. It has proved serviceable through many differing situations. Political leaders have come and gone, but the Constitution remains.

Christians also have their written guarantees. The faithful believer has always had written assurances since the time when Moses penned what we know today as the first five books of the Bible. After Moses other prophets and apostles have written other books, and together they comprise the Holy Scriptures. Church leaders have come and gone, but the Holy Scriptures remain so that Christians can see for themselves what God wants them to know and what special privileges He has given them. The Bible has become so important to both Jews and Christians that both groups have been called followers of the Book. They have even been accused of bibliolatry, worship of the Book. The place of honor in a Jewish synagog is reserved for the Torah, the books written by Moses.

High regard for God's written Word was commanded by God Himself. The books of Moses were to be placed in the Ark of the Covenant along with other sacred symbols taken from Jewish history. This ark was sprinkled with the blood of the atonement to signify its place in God's covenant relationship with His people and then placed in the Holy of Holies, a place so sacred in the tabernacle or temple that it could only be entered once a year by the high priest.

At times the Hebrews forgot about the God who had made them a nation, but the Book was always there calling them back. By this Book prophets sent by God to the people substantiated their call, and it was from this Book that they preached repentance. If a prophet preached a message found to be at variance with the Book, he was considered a false prophet. Even our Lord Jesus Christ put Himself under the authority of the Book when He said that He had come not to destroy but to fulfill what Moses and the prophets had written. The apostles of Jesus, in preaching to the Jews, went to great pains to show that the message of Jesus was not a new religion but only the old religion of the Book brought to its final and ultimate conclusion.

Christians and Jews do not need to be reminded that they have frequently disregarded God's requirements set down for them in the Holy Scriptures. Regardless of how the Scriptures have been treated, they are always waiting there to be studied and examined so that God's will and plan can be discovered. St. Paul says of the Jews who do not accept Jesus as the Christ that they have a veil over their eyes when they read the Old Testament Scriptures so that they do not see Him there. Something similar happened in the medieval church, which had the New Testament Scriptures but failed to comprehend that these sacred writings teach salvation by grace through faith without works. In both cases the institutional church preserved the Scriptures but without understanding their message.

No one would dare suggest that the *Book of Concord* is on the same level as the Holy Scriptures. But the *Book of Concord* has faithfully preserved basic Scriptural teachings and has applied them to problems confronted by the church. If we want to know how the apostles and prophets faced their problems, we can read the Holy Scriptures. If we want to know how the church after the days of the apostles faced its problems, we can look into the *Book of Concord*.

Since 1580 Lutherans have frequently forgotten what it means to be *Lutherans*. But there stood the *Book of Concord* to remind them of what their church stands for. In the 1700s Lutherans, like many other European Christians, had surrendered their faith to the arguments of the rationalists, who denied miracles and anything supernatural. However, with the tricentennial celebrations of the posting of the Ninety-Five Theses in 1817 and the signing of the Augsburg Confession in 1830, some Lutherans began an intensive study of the works of Luther and the Lutheran Confessions. Such research provided the seedbed for the confessional awakening in which The Lutheran Church—Missouri Synod and The American Lutheran Church had their roots. What happened with the rediscovery of Lutheranism in the early 1800s was not unlike King Josiah's discovery of the Books of Moses or Martin Luther's discovery of the doctrine of justification in the Bible.

The year 1980, the 400th anniversary of the publication of the *Book of Concord*, might under God's grace provide the kind of confessional reawakening the church has experienced before. What blessings might result if throughout Lutheranism—on every level—the Lutheran Confessions and their theology would receive the attention they deserve! Roman Catholics have years of jubilee in which their faithful can travel to Rome and renew and refresh their allegiance to that church. Lutherans could make 1980 a year of jubilee in which our faithful can take a spiritual pilgrimage into our church's charter documents.

Some will object to this kind of celebration because they consider it devotion to a book, bibliolatry. Living relationships, they will assert, can exist only between persons and not between a person and a book. Christians will agree that devotion must be directed to Jesus Christ alone, but this is not devotion to a solitary figure standing outside of history, of whom we know little or nothing. The devotion is directed to everything Christ did and said. True love for Him encompasses strict adherence to His teachings, and these are found only in the Holy Scriptures. We are not confronted with an either-or when we face Jesus and the Scriptures, but it is through the Scriptures that we find Jesus.

Lutherans are going to look at their Confessions as a way to see the light of the Holy Scriptures shining through into their situation. The heroic faith of Martin Luther and the other reformers will awaken admiration even among those who cannot accept their teachings. But a festival commemorating Lutheran beliefs does not center in admiration for these men but in *what* they stood for. The *Book of Concord* tells us this. Thus our celebration of the 400th anniversary of the *Book of Concord* is not merely noting a historical marker, but it is our involvement in the faith confessed there,

11

along with our personal pledge and commitment to it.

The *Book of Concord* comprises 11 separate or individual documents, each unique and different from the others. Here is their listing in the generally accepted chronological order (their order in the *Book of Concord* and in this volume is somewhat different). The Apostles' Creed, whose form as used today comes from the eighth century, can be traced back to the second century, when it was used in the city of Rome at the time of baptism. The Nicene Creed is the product of church councils held in 325 and 381. Most hidden are the origins of the Athanasian Creed, first used in liturgies and sermons. Long thought to come from the eighth century, it is now dated as early as the sixth century. Both the Small Catechism and Large Catechism were readied for publication in 1529 by their author, Dr. Martin Luther. The Small Catechism was instruction especially for the laity. The Large Catechism is a collection of Luther's reedited sermons. From the hand of Luther's co-worker, Philip Melanchthon, comes the Augsburg Confession, which was presented at an official assembly of the Holy Roman Empire in 1530. The Apology is the author's own defense of the Augsburg Confession. It was begun in Augsburg in 1530 and completed the next year in Wittenberg. The Smalcald Articles were prepared by Luther in 1536 for a meeting of theologians and princes in 1537 in preparation for a united Lutheran defense at a council called by the pope. Melanchthon authored the Treatise on the Power and Primacy of the Pope, officially adopted at that same meeting at Smalcald. The Formula of Concord evolved through several prior documents including sermons, theses, and condensations during the period after Luther's death. The final form dates from 1577. Often overlooked as a separate confession is the Preface to the *Book of Concord*, which appeared with its publication in 1580.

When Lutherans say they accept these 11 documents as adequate statements of their faith, they are not suggesting in any way that they are divinely inspired. They are not making any judgment on documents not accepted as official confessions. They are not stating that the literary merit of the official confessions is superior to other writings. For example, the *Te Deum*, part of the traditional Matins liturgy, is both a literary and a theological masterpiece; most Christians could subscribe it without hesitation. Yet it has never received official confessional recognition. The question must be examined: What qualities make one document an official confession and another not?

Everything a Christian says or writes about his faith is a confession. This is especially applicable to pastors, who publicly represent the faith of their congregations, and to church leaders of large organizational units like synods and denominations. Sermons are examples of confessional statements of faith which most of us hear regularly. The sermon is an exposition of the Word of God to the people, but it also serves as a confession of the pastor's faith. Anyone lacking such confessional confidence and certainty should not preach.

Since the apostles acknowledged Jesus as the Christ, the Christian church has been filled with confessors. They can be well-known persons like Peter or they can be children expressing their faith to their parents. They can be Christians martyred by Roman emperors or captives in a Soviet prison camp. Confessions made under such stress tell us that the church is still alive. Where confessions cease, there it can be assumed that the church is dead. We could, if we wanted to, take all the confessions that have ever been made and place them into one large book. Not only would such a collection be unwieldly, the confessions in the collection would repeat themselves in words and thoughts. Christians do have, as St. Paul says, "one Lord, *one faith.*"

With such a mammoth collection of confessions, we would soon ask ourselves why we couldn't condense and unify them. This would make it easier to tell the world what the church believes. It would make it easier to determine if the Christians were really agreed among themselves. The use of the same creeds would indicate that the same faith was being confessed. It was this natural desire for uniformity that brought our Apostles' Creed into its final form. At first there were many creeds, each church having its own form. As churches had closer contact with one another one uniform creed naturally emerged.

Not only is the drive for uniformity a motive in making some documents creeds, but the time of a document is also crucial. For a document to become confessional it has to be the right document, at the right time, and at the right place. During the Reformation, Luther was the recognized leader, but it was Melanchthon's Augsburg Confession which became the basic confession of the Lutheran Church. It was the right document, at the right time, and at the right place.

The Augsburg Confession became confessionally significant from the moment it was presented. Other documents were at first considered to be insignificant, but were recognized as having confessional merit at a later time.

Important for Lutherans in marking the 400th anniversary of the *Book of Concord* is that the confessors' faith in these pages makes our church *Lutheran*. Each denomination has its own history and system of Christian thought. Generally there is a mark or trait that distinguishes one denomination from another. Roman Catholics are recognized for their allegiance to the pope. Episcopalians are associated with the use of the *Book of Common Prayer* and their system of bishops. The Eastern Orthodox center their religion around tradition, the Divine Liturgy, and the prominent use of icons in worship. But what is the distinctive mark of Lutherans?

The unique characteristic of the Lutheran Church is its allegiance to the documents known as the Lutheran Confessions. Other Christian denominations have confessions, but they do not play such an important role. Not every Lutheran group accepts each and every confession contained in the *Book of Concord*, but most Lutheran groups refuse to accept as doctrine any position condemned by these Confessions. In the United States each major Lutheran group makes mention of these Confessions in its constitution. This is also true of most European Lutheran churches.

Americans celebrated the 200th anniversary of the nation in 1976, and it seems unlikely that they will let 1983 (the 200th anniversary of the Constitution) slip by unnoticed. An appropriate way of marking such an occasion would be a concentrated effort in the nation's schools to study the Constitution and related historical documents. The 400th anniversary of the *Book of Concord* in 1980 can hold out to the Lutheran Church a similar promise. Confessional revival can occur when the church studies its roots and is refreshed with the nourishment which only they can supply. For Lutherans these confessional roots are found in the *Book of Concord* and ultimately in the Holy Scriptures as the written Word of God. Our purpose in such study can only be to make our commitment more firm so that we are enabled to proclaim the forgiveness of sins for the sake of Jesus Christ. To this proclamation the year of Lutheran jubilee and celebration, 1980, should be dedicated.

II. How It All Started— The Biblical Origins

Many organizations have initiation rituals for new members. The church also has rituals which inform future members about its purposes and what it expects of them. Those accepted into the Lutheran Church are asked not only if they accept the Bible as God's Word but also whether they hold to the teachings of the Lutheran Church as they are set forth in the Lutheran Confessions. The wording can vary, but the intent and purpose remain the same.

The Lutheran interest in confessions is strongly connected with the belief that the truth of God can be set forth clearly in written statements and that it can be passed down from one generation to another. Written confessions are a means to make certain that God's truth will not be altered. It was for the same reason that God caused His Word to be written down in the Holy Scriptures.

It would be misleading to suggest that confessions are a Lutheran invention. Not only have Christian confessions been associated with the historic Christian church, but they make up a vital part of the lives of God's people in both Old and New Testaments. St. Paul viewed confession as so necessary that he wrote:

> Because if you confess with your lips that Jesus is Lord and believe in your heart that God raised Him from the dead, you will be saved. For man believes with his heart and so is justified, and he confesses with his lips and so is saved (Rom. 10:9-10).

Making one's confession in Jesus as Lord was not an option for the first Christians, but on their confession hinged their personal salvation.

All groups and not just churches have "confessions," statements containing the reasons for formation of their organizations and why they continue to exist. Neighborhood improvement associations, political parties, labor unions, credit unions, book clubs—all have statements setting forth their organizational goals and purposes. Groups that lose or forget their original goals either disintegrate or have to forge new goals for themselves in order to survive. The confessions of a church give the reasons for that church's existence. Whenever a church's sense of its own confession grows dim, that church begins to lose its sense of direction and to grow weak internally. Its outward shell may remain, but there is little life in the center.

Adam and Eve were created by God to be confessional creatures. Among all the creatures made by God only they had God's image and were so structured in their inner being that they could voluntarily return to God the glory in which they had been created. Confession may be defined as returning to God the glory in which man was created. In humanity's original state, confession was not a Sunday activity as it is today when Christians gather to recite the Apostles' Creed. Confession was as much a part of the first man and woman as breathing and eating. Their entire existence was confessional. There was no moment in their life when they were not returning glory to God. Their constant confessional existence, however, was brought to an abrupt end by sin. They reversed the divine scheme by giving glory to themselves and not to God. In attempting to make themselves equal with God, they renounced the confession that God was their Creator. The attempt to unseat God, of course, was a total failure. Instead of gaining their goal of equality with God, Adam and Eve lost the ability to respond confessionally to God's glory. They were no longer God's children. This estrangement from God meant that confessional response was impossible.

Since God's glory no longer could be reflected in them, people began a new existence in which they manufactured their own gods. The God who had created them as confessional creatures had no more real existence for them. Their rebellious act had morally blinded them so they could no longer see God's constant and continued glory in the creation. They had perverted themselves so that response to the true God, the Creator, had become impossible. False religions sprang up as ill-starred attempts to make confession, but people found their goals not in the Creator but in the creature. Men and women had lost the original content of their confession and were filling the empty void and the religious vacuum in their lives with their own inventions.

God in an act of pure mercy and grace permitted His glory to shine through again to humanity so that in the darkness which they had made for themselves people could once again respond confessionally to the Creator God. The promise that one of Eve's sons would relieve her from the predicament for which she was responsible provided her with enough hope that she could again respond confessionally. At the birth of her first son she confessed: "I have gotten a man, the LORD" (Gen. 4:1 Beck). With that statement began the history of Christian confession. The content of Eve's confession has been absolutely basic to the faith of God's people ever since then. Never did the Jews, God's people in the Old Testament, live without confessing their hope that Eve's Son and her Deliverer would come. Today God's people, the church, confess that this Deliverer has come in the person of Jesus of Nazareth. This confession is repeated whenever the church speaks of Jesus as the Christ (the Anointed One). The simple abbreviation for this confession is "Jesus Christ," a phrase so common that many have never realized that it is a confession about Jesus.

The church today still confesses what the Old Testament people of God did. Along with their belief that God's promised Deliverer, the Messiah, would come from their people, the Jews confessed that God was one and that this one God had created the universe. This fundamental belief of the Old Testament constitutes the Apostles' Creed's first statement: "I believe in God, the Father almighty, maker of heaven and earth." But what is so commonplace to Christian faith today was rarely acknowledged by ancient peoples. The religious literature emanating from the two great centers of ancient culture (Egypt and the Tigris-Euphrates valley) is replete with an endless cluttering of gods. The later civilizations of the Greeks and Romans provided no relief from the oversupply of gods. The one bit of monotheism briefly appearing in Egypt identified the one god with the sun. The gods of the ancient people either were associated with the cycles in nature or were mere projections of the people themselves. In time atheistic cynics ridiculed these man-made gods and goddesses.

Right in the middle of this polytheistic confusion the

pious Jew made the first verses of Genesis his own confession: "In the beginning God created the heavens and the earth." The God revealed in the pages of the Old Testament was not creaturely in any respect, as were the polytheistic imitations. Here was a God who was no creature, but who was different, separate, and superior to His creation. He was the sovereign Creator, to whom all creatures owed thankful allegiance for their creation. This God also was one, and His power was not divided among others. The belief that God is one is called monotheism, a belief still essential to Christianity as it is to Judaism. Today's Jew still confesses as his fathers have done for 3,500 years: "Hear, O Israel, the Lord our God is one Lord" (Deut. 6:4). From the call of Abraham to the destruction of Jerusalem, the faith of God's people was constantly threatened by polytheism. In the midst of this threat, the Jew could cling to this confession, called the *Shema*, that God is one. The basic religion of the Old Testament could be outlined in three principles: the oneness of God, His creation of all things, and His promise to bring salvation to the world through Someone born from the Jewish people.

These three Old Testament principles served as the foundation for Christianity as it was revealed in the New Testament. Christians thought of themselves as Abraham's descendants. The church regarded itself as God's true Israel and kept the Jewish confession as its own. What really made the difference between the Old and New Testaments was that the Christians saw in Jesus of Nazareth the answer to God's promises. The pious Jew knew that God would send a Deliverer. Eve had looked for Him, and finding Him was the hope of all God's faithful in the Old Testament. When the first Christians heard what Jesus said of Himself and saw the miracles He performed, they were convinced that He was that special Someone through whom God would bring redemption. A high point in the gospel history was Peter's confession in which he recognized Jesus as the fulfillment of all the Old Testament promises: "You are the Christ, the Son of the living God" (Matt. 16:16). The Creator God against whom man had sinned had fulfilled His promise of coming to man's aid in the Person of His Son. The early church's confessional life now focused on the Person of Jesus. No one could enter the Christian community without making the confession that Jesus was the Lord or Christ, the One who had been with the Father before the Creation. Paul wrapped all the essential elements of the Old Testament faith around the Person of Jesus in a reformulated confession:

> Hence, as to the eating of food offered to idols, we know that "an idol has no real existence," and that "there is no God but one." For although there may be so-called gods in heaven or on earth—as indeed there are many "gods" and many "lords"—yet for us there is one God, the Father, from whom are all things and for whom we exist, and one Lord, Jesus Christ, through whom are all things and through whom we exist" (1 Cor. 8:4-6).

Christianity was not a reversion to paganism or polytheism. The Christian confession was a restatement of the Old Testament faith. This restatement was required by the appearance of the Creator God in the Person of the Father's Son, Jesus. Him the church confessed as Lord and Christ. Most of the New Testament is written to convince us that Jesus is both Lord and Christ. From the very beginning, right after Jesus' resurrection, the apostles proclaimed this message with the hope that others would join them in this confession. The Book of Acts tells us of their successes and some of their failures in this task. Bringing their readers to make this confession was the goal of each apostolic sermon. Many of the church's earliest confessions can be found in the pages of the New Testament. These confessions, used from the very beginning of the early church, not only saw in Jesus the answer to the prophets' hope but recognized Him as both divine and human. It was in His humanity that He endured a death for sins upon the cross, and to announce that He had satisfied divine wrath God glorified Him through the resurrection from the dead.

One of the most beautiful creeds confessing our Lord's suffering and the Father's glorification of Him is recorded by Paul in his Letter to Philippi:

> Have this mind among yourselves, which is yours in Christ Jesus, who, though He was in the form of God, did not count equality with God a thing to be grasped, but emptied Himself, taking the form of a servant, being born in the likeness of men. And being found in human form He humbled Himself and became obedient unto death, even death on a cross. Therefore God has highly exalted Him and bestowed on Him the name which is above every name, that at the name of Jesus every knee should bow, in heaven and on earth, and

every tongue confess that Jesus Christ is Lord, to the glory of God the Father (Phil. 2:5-11).

Such a beautifully worded creed might have been sung to melodies in the worship services of the early Christians. This creed confesses that in the first part of our Lord's life He was debased in suffering and that in the second part He was exalted in glory by God His Father. These two divisions are still maintained in the Apostles' and Nicene Creeds. In the examination for confirmation, children in the Lutheran Church are still asked about the two stages in our Lord's life. The confessional answer of the second chapter of Philippians is still made: humiliation and exaltation. The church's faith expressed in its confession has not changed during the past 1,900 years. But it was not Paul or the Philippians who first set the pattern of seeing in the life of Jesus periods of humiliation and exaltation, but Jesus Himself. Frequently in the gospels is recorded His own prediction that first the Son of Man must die before He should enter His glory through the Resurrection.

The church grew rapidly in the second half of the first century. There is evidence in the New Testament that each of the territorial churches developed its own creeds. These creeds were natural expressions of their faith. Some churches may have used more than one creed. The simplest creed was "Jesus is Lord" (1 Cor. 12:3). Others, as we have seen, spoke about the relationship of Jesus to the Father or about the atoning work of Jesus. Creedal wordings were different, but their meanings were the same. And each time the early Christians gathered to confess that Jesus was Lord, they were aware that their confession was motivated by the Holy Spirit. Remember that Paul had said: "No one can say 'Jesus is Lord' except by the Holy Spirit" (1 Cor. 12:3).

There was a time in the life of each Christian when he made a confession of the triune God. The church did not have a word like "triune" or "Trinity" till around the third century, but the early Christians did know God by the name 'Father and Son and Holy Spirit." At the end of Matthew's gospel there is the record that Jesus gave command to make disciples out of the nations by baptizing them in this name for God. Baptism was never administered without a confession. From this connection between Baptism and confession there grew the custom of asking the candidate for Baptism if he believed in the Father, the Son, and the Holy Spirit. His affirmative response contained the seeds for the three parts of the Apostles' and Nicene Creeds used by Christians to this day. The baptismal confession was never forgotten but renewed, repeated, and celebrated each time baptized Christians would gather for worship. The congregation which gathered to hear God's Word read and preached and to receive the Supper of Jesus was the assembly of the baptized. Their recitation of the creed was just another opportunity to reanswer the questions first addressed to them at Baptism. In a very explicit way the confession originally made at Baptism is repeated at any church service that begins with the words "In the name of the Father and of the Son and of the Holy Spirit."

It is not an option for Christians to make confessions of their faith. It is required. Seared into the Christian conscience are these very definite and positive words of Jesus:

> So everyone who acknowledges [confesses] Me before men, I also will acknowledge [confess] before My Father who is in heaven; but whoever denies Me before men, I also will deny before My Father who is in heaven (Matt. 10:32-33).

These words contain promise and threat about the necessity of the church's confessional life. Let's put it like this: Each time we make confession of our faith, Jesus stands before His Father. If we say that He is Lord and Christ, He will acknowledge before His Father that we belong to Him. Should we refuse to do this, He will have to tell His Father that we really don't belong to Him. Confessing the name of Jesus is a very serious matter. It has repercussions in heaven as well as on earth.

The apostle St. Peter has already been singled out for his great confession that Jesus is the Christ, the Son of the living God. It should be remembered, however, that Peter is also singled out for his great denial. All four of our gospel writers include the episode of how the great confessor became the great denier. Not only could he no longer say that Jesus is the Christ, he could not even say that he was acquainted with Jesus. We all know how Peter repented and that Jesus restored to him his high and important position among the apostles. The account of Peter's denial was not recorded that we should despise Peter, but rather as a warning that every Christian, bar none, lives under the constant threat of satanic power to deny Jesus.

At the end of his life the apostle Paul was greatly concerned that Timothy should maintain the faith of the Christian church which he had learned from Paul himself and that he should never be shaken in his confession. Paul knew that he would not be around much longer to encourage Timothy and bolster him up in difficult times. Christianity had not even passed the half-century mark at this time, but many of the early church leaders had already deserted the faith. At this pungent moment Paul reminded Timothy of the confession he had made when he assumed the obligations of a pastor and asked him to view it in the light of Jesus' own confession before Pontius Pilate. Our Lord had been asked by the Roman governor at His trial if He were a king. A denial of kingship would have meant immediate release for Jesus. But He chose to confess the truth about Himself that He indeed was a king. That confession meant death for our Lord and made Him the first of many martyrs, people who die for having confessed their faith. At the head of all these confessors and martyrs stands Jesus. Paul urges Timothy to take Jesus as his example:

> Fight the good fight of faith; take hold of the eternal life to which you were called when you made the good confession in the presence of many witnesses. In the presence of God who gives life to all things, and of Christ Jesus who in His testimony before Pontius Pilate made the good confession, I charge you . . . (1 Tim. 6:12-14).

Confession runs like a thread from the church's establishment to its final consummation when Jesus takes it to Himself. When He comes in glory, even those who have obstinately and persistently denied Him will have to acknowledge who He really is. Paul said to the Philippians that every knee will bow in heaven and on earth and every tongue will confess that Jesus is Lord, to the glory of God the Father. As the church takes as her example the confession of her suffering Lord before Pilate, she also sees her glorified Lord appearing at the last day, urging the church forward to its final glory and reward. Speaking of this future glory Paul continues to tell Timothy:

> I charge you to keep the commandment unstained and free from reproach until the appearing of our Lord Jesus Christ; and this will be made manifest at the proper time by the blessed and only Sovereign, the King of kings and Lord of lords, who alone has immortality and dwells in unap-

proachable light, whom no man has ever seen or can see. To Him be honor and eternal dominion. Amen. (1 Tim. 6:14-16).

With words like these the church left the early period in which—unlike any other time—it enjoyed the immediate supervision of the Lord's apostles. It was a jolting experience not unlike the feeling when a child first leaves home. The apostles themselves had experienced this feeling of personal emptiness when Jesus told them He could no longer be with them. Now the apostles would no longer personally be with the church. But it was not the personal presence of Jesus or the apostles that really mattered. What mattered was if each subsequent generation would hear the words of Jesus urging Christians to confess. No one will deny that there were dark days for the church after apostolic times. But in that darkness confessional fires were lit and the glow from those lights has never gone out. The first of these lights in a long series was the Apostles' Creed.

III. The Catholic Tradition

Because of the strong influence of Martin Luther's experience with the Roman *Catholic* Church, the Lutheran Church has had a slight aversion to the use of the word "catholic" in its creeds, hymns, and liturgies. To most Lutherans this word is synonymous with the Roman Catholic Church, against whose views they have protested from the very beginning of the Reformation. But personal dislike cannot cover up the historical fact that the three oldest creeds in Christendom—the Apostles', the Nicene, the Athanasian— all use the word "catholic" to describe the church. All three creeds state that part of our confession is that we believe in the catholic church. At the time when these three creeds came into existence, none of their formulators were thinking exclusively of the Roman Catholic Church by this phrase, but they were thinking of the entire church of Jesus Christ spread throughout the world. Universal, spread throughout the world, is what the word "catholic" originally meant and by itself is what it still means. The first three creeds, the Apostles', Nicene, and Athanasian, were called catholic creeds because they were used in so many places and not just in one church or one place. They have never been the private possession of one set or group of believers but belong to Christians throughout the world.

To this day these creeds are used by Christians who have gathered under the banners of different and opposing denominations. In spite of the many divisions in the outward fabric of Christianity and its century-long history of differences, these confessions point to a common heritage for most Christians. The hymnals and worship books of most churches contain one or more of these creeds. When attending other churches on special occasions, many Lutherans have discovered this for themselves when browsing through the hymnals and prayer books in the racks attached to the backs of pews. Most Lutherans are accustomed to reciting the

Apostles' Creed from memory and have little difficulty with the Nicene Creed. These creeds are as much a part of their religious fiber as is the Lord's Prayer. Since these creeds have their roots in the history of the church as far back as postapostolic times, Lutherans and all other Christians using them participate in the same catholic tradition stretching back over 19 centuries. As Christians are attached to the same common roots in the past, they are also attached to one another. Wherever there is a Christian culture, regardless of the language being used, there on a Sunday morning one of the catholic creeds is likely to be employed to express the people's faith. These catholic creeds maintain a vertical relationship with churches in the past and a horizontal connection between various churches in the present. Where they are recited, there is the one church for which Jesus died and which He through His Holy Spirit established and still maintains.

Wherever denominations differing among themselves share a formal allegiance to these catholic creeds, they at least have some type of platform from which they can work to possible unity. Today when Lutherans discuss their faith with Roman Catholics, Presbyterians, Episcopalians, and Eastern Orthodox, their mutual discussions can in some way take into account their common allegiance to one or all of the catholic creeds. Interpretations of the creeds differ in some cases, but there is general agreement on their formal wording. When the Lutherans prepared their unique confessions in the 1500s, they made it clear to their opponents in the Roman Catholic Church that they agreed with them on the acceptance of the catholic creeds. Roman Catholics on their part have recognized the Lutheran position toward these creeds as similar to their own. It is important to see how each of the catholic creeds came into existence and how it has been used in the church.

The Apostles' Creed

The most widely used of the three creeds is the Apostles' Creed. In spite of a few stylistic differences, the form used in most churches is identical. Besides its regular use in worship services, it is generally used at the time of Baptism, and for this reason is called the baptismal creed. It is also used to prepare catechumens for fuller membership in the church through Holy Communion. Martin Luther included it in both the Small and the Large Catechism. It is mentioned by name in the first two officially recognized Lutheran Confessions of the 1500s, the Augsburg Confession and the Apology. It is also listed in the Formula of Concord as a confession of the church. Thus Lutherans, who value church history, give it a prominent place.

Scholars point out that the Apostles' Creed in its final form as used today comes from the 700s. But this information fails to point out how old the Apostles' Creed really is. There is a striking similarity to it in the following passage from the New Testament:

> For Christ also *died for sins* once for all, the righteous for the unrighteous, that He might bring us to God, being put to death in the flesh but made alive in the spirit; *in which He went and preached to the spirits in prison*. . . . Baptism, which corresponds to this, now saves you, not as a removal of dirt from the body but as an appeal to God for a clear conscience, through the *resurrection* of Jesus Christ, who *has gone into heaven* and is at the *right hand of God*, with angels, authorities, and powers subject to Him (1 Peter 3:18-22).

Underlined here are those parts perpetuated in the Apostles' Creed: Christ died, He went to the prison—we would say "He descended to hell"—He rose, He ascended to heaven, and He sat down at God's right hand.

Already in the 100s creeds that resembled the Apostles' Creed were used in Christian churches everywhere throughout the Roman Empire. Remember that this was hardly a century after the time of Jesus and not long after the death of John, the last surviving apostle. Unless we would listen very carefully to the recitation of these earlier creeds, we would scarcely notice any difference between one of them and the Apostles' Creed we use. For example, the one used in Rome around the year 150 has a remarkable similarity to our version, 1,800 years later. That's antiquity! Here is my own translation of that creed:

> I believe in God the Father Almighty.
> And in Christ Jesus, His only Son, our Lord, who was conceived by the Holy Ghost and Mary the Virgin, crucified under Pontius Pilate and was buried, on the third day rose from the dead, ascended into heaven, was seated at the right hand of the Father, from there He shall come to judge the living and the dead.
> And in the Holy Spirit, the holy Church, the forgiveness of sins, the resurrection of the flesh. Amen.

If a time machine would take us back 1,800 years to the city of Rome, to one of the houses where the Christians worshipped or to one of those underground caves used for the burial of the dead, called catacombs, we would feel right at home when this creed was recited during the worship service. The language used at that time was Greek. But here is a universality in the confession of faith that has not been destroyed by time or place.

Creeds do not come into existence because some experts in religion, called theologians, decide that it would be a nice idea for the church to have a new creed or confession. Confessions come into existence as the church's answer to pressing needs and dangers. Most of the problems that have afflicted the church have centered around the Person and the work of the church's Founder, Jesus Christ Himself. When a false teaching, a heresy, confronts the church, it is met by the church's corporate faith in a frontal counterattack called a confession. Against false teaching, confession is not only the best but finally the only weapon in the church's arsenal. It is both the first and the last line of defense. False teaching gives the church an opportunity to confess what it has always believed. In this sense, any true confession is not really new.

Christians are known for confessing that Jesus is both God and man. Of all doctrines this is the most delicately balanced. If either Christ's deity or His humanity is emphasized to the exclusion of the other, or only overshadowing the other, the church is well on the way to a perversion of everything it believes. In the next section, on the Nicene Creed, we will see that the danger confronted there was understanding Jesus solely as a creature, to the total exclusion of understanding Him as God. However, the problem of the first and second centuries, the one handled in the Apostles' Creed, was just the reverse. Some who called themselves Christians recognized Jesus as God but did not really believe that He was man in every respect. Through the forerunners of the Apostles' Creed the Christians of those days responded in confession to this danger which, left uncorrected, would have brought down the infant church. A word about this false understanding must be said.

Sometime toward the end of the first century there began to circulate throughout the Christian church a belief that God had not actually become a man in the Person of Jesus Christ. There is nearly universal agreement that this false idea crept

into the church through Greek philosophical thought. A few
centuries before, a Greek philosopher by the name of Plato, a
student of the famous Socrates, had propagated the view that
"spirit," things without matter or material substance, were
good and that "matter," physical things, were evil. Such views
were very influential and were further developed by other
philosophers well into the Christian era. It was almost
inevitable that some of the early Christians would understand
the Christian message from this popular but quite false
philosophical point of view. To be sure, Jesus Himself had
spoken of sinful mankind in estrangement from God as
"flesh" and the realm of His Father and the redeemed as
"spirit." But in no way was He adopting Plato's philosophical
idea of "spirit" with its superiority over things with physical
substance. By "spirit" Jesus did not mean ghostly objects, but
He meant the realm ruled by the Holy Spirit. Those born of the
Spirit were people in whom the Holy Spirit had worked the
conviction of personal sin and the awareness that Jesus is the
Christ.

Quite opposed to Plato's philosophy, Christianity had
followed the Old Testament religion in regarding the
material world highly. The world whose creation was
described in Genesis was a physical, material world, not a
spiritual one. Part of the Christian message was that the
created world would be freed from its current bondage to sin
to be reconstituted on the last day to a fuller glory than it had
ever known. Indeed, the first article of Christian faith is that
God is the Creator of heaven and earth. Faith in the
resurrection of the dead showed even further how highly
Christians treasured God's material creation. After the
Christian's death his soul or spirit would survive in the
presence of Christ, but the truly glorious moment would
come with the resurrection of the body.

Jesus' teachings on body and spirit were clear, but
nevertheless some in the church understood His words as if
they had come from a philosopher influenced by Plato.
Already in the time of the apostles this false thinking was at
work. Some Christians in Corinth had denied the resurrection of the body, but St. Paul was successful in handling that
situation. But at the end of the first century the problem had
become more critical. Now some were denying the Incarnation, the doctrine that God had become man in the Person of
Jesus. If this false belief which saw matter as evil had

survived, Christianity would have collapsed and what remained would have been just another philosophy, one with little use for Christianity's historical substance.

During this critical time at the end of the first century, it seems that John was the last survivor of our Lord's apostles. It is apparent that he wrote his Gospel and three letters, all of which bear his name and are incorporated in our New Testament, as loud and vigorous protests against this denial of the Incarnation. John wrote bluntly: "And the Word became *flesh*" (John 1:14). At the end of the same Gospel the apostle includes the account of the resurrected Jesus inviting the unbelieving Thomas to put his fingers and hands into the wounds caused by the crucifixion to demonstrate the material reality of His resurrection.

It was in this climate at the time of John that the Apostles' Creed first had its origins in several creeds. These earliest of creeds have three parts, one for each of the Persons of the Holy Trinity, but the emphasis is always on the second part, the one centering in the Person of Jesus. This does not mean that the early Christians did not confess the Father and the Holy Spirit. They certainly did just that. They were indeed Trinitarian. Take a look at the creed of Rome. But in order to give a clear confession about the Person of Jesus, especially His humanity, the second section of the three-part creeds, the one on Jesus, is the longest.

If the Apostles' Creed or one of its ancient forerunners like the creed of Rome is laid out word for word, it soon becomes evident that most of the short phrases handle episodes in the life of Jesus. These episodes can be divided into two sections, one dealing with our Lord's life of humiliation and the other with His exaltation, just as is done in Philippians 2. The purpose of this was to state before all men, especially the deniers, that the Son of God had come in the flesh, lived our kind of life, and died our kind of death. John in his Second Letter spoke quite directly to this issue sometime around the year 90, when he wrote that certain deceivers "will not acknowledge the coming of Jesus Christ in the flesh" (2 John 7).

The need to confront this problem was met in the earliest forms of the Apostles' Creed by stating that the One conceived by the Holy Spirit through Mary, the same One who was crucified and buried and then rose from the dead, was the Son of God Himself. No separation between the divine and human natures was to be tolerated in any way. Especially in regard to the crucifixion the unity of the two natures had to be made absolutely clear. The One on the cross was not just the man Jesus of Nazareth, but the God-man Jesus Christ.

The Apostles' Creed along with its forerunners nailed down the unity of natures with the words "only" as used in "His *only* Son" and "under Pontius Pilate" as used in "crucified under Pontius Pilate." The word "only" in the creed is deceptively small and apparently insignificant. But in reality the entire meaning of the creed hinges on this one little word. Most English versions of the creed translate this word with the slightly longer "only begotten" as in "His only begotten Son." This might have more punch than using just the word "only," but it is still not quite good enough. That word "only" translates the very important Greek word *monogenes*, which by itself means "one of a kind." John alone applies it to Jesus in the first and third chapters of his Gospel. Remember that John shared the same concerns as did the early creeds about those who denied that the Son of God had actually become a real human being. John uses this word *monogenes* in speaking of the Incarnation: "And the Word became flesh and dwelt among us, full of grace and truth; we have beheld His glory, glory as of the *only* Son from the Father" (John 1:14). He uses the word again a few verses later: "No one has ever seen God; the *only* Son, who is in the bosom of the Father, He has made Him known" (John 1:18). It is used in the famous passage John 3:16-18: "For God so loved the world that He gave His *only* Son, that whoever believes in Him should not perish but have eternal life. . . . He who believes in Him is not condemned; he who does not believe is condemned already, because he has not believed in the name of the *only* Son of God." That word "only," *monogenes*, was brought into the Apostles' Creed. It refers to the One who alone possesses God's glory and who alone as God is the only one who has seen God. He is the only one whom the Father has sent for the sacrifice of the world's sins, and outside of Him there is no salvation. With the word "only" the Apostles' Creed says all these things.

The other hinge phrase in the creed is "under Pontius Pilate." All the forerunners of the Apostles' Creed now available to us refer to the Roman procurator Pontius Pialte. Some add the names of Herod, the vassal king of Galilee before whom Jesus appeared shortly before His crucifixion, and of Tiberius Caesar, the reigning Roman emperor at that time. Some morally concerned Christians have been annoyed that the name of a political opportunist and moral jellyfish like Pontius Pilate should be included in something as sacred as the church's creed. But Pilate is not mentioned because Christians see anything exemplary in his life. It is not the purpose of the Apostle's Creed to set moral examples for Christians. Still, it was very basic to the early Christians to say that Jesus had been "crucified under Pontius Pilate." With this phrase they were saying with a loud, clear voice that the Son of God had had an earthly existence that could be measured off by the same kind of calendar days that had marked off the existence of a man like Pontius Pilate or any other human being. In this way the doctrine of the Incarnation was reaffirmed. We can have the same historical certainty about Jesus that we can have about any figure in history. This means that Jesus did not live out there in some kind of spiritual space. He lived on earth, and He lived a real life.

The Christian church in the 20th century is still troubled by those who try to separate the divine and human in Jesus, the same problem that caused trouble in the first and second centuries. Today some teach that we should believe in Christ or the Son of God but doubt the historical or earthly character of Jesus' life. In spite of all the historical doubts they raise about Jesus, they still urge belief in Him. This is an incredible contradiction, which the apostle John saw already at his time as destructive of the faith. The Apostles' Creed in its earliest forms was directed specifically to this error of separating the divine and human in Jesus or putting a higher value on one than on the other. Since the same problem has recurred, the Apostles' Creed is as serviceable and valuable today as it was when it first came into existence. Here is an example of how our creeds are catholic or universal in their outlook. They break through the provincial and parochial surroundings in which they arose and are capable of addressing problems of much wider scope.

There is general agreement that there was no one author of the Apostles' Creed. Not only is it the most catholic creed in the sense that it had the widest use under several different forms in the early church; it is catholic in that no one man or one part of the church can claim exclusive authorship of it. The Apostles' Creed deserves to be called *the* creed of the church, the *entire* church. No one denomination can claim it as its unique possession, and thus today it maintains its glorious catholicity.

As early as the year 390 it was given the name Apostles' Creed, *symbolum apostolicum*. During the Middle Ages a legend circulated about its origin which was widely accepted. The story that each of the 12 apostles contributed a phrase to the creed:

> On the tenth day after the Ascension, when the disciples were gathered together for fear of the Jews, the Lord sent the promised Paraclete upon them. At His coming they were inflamed like red-hot iron, and being filled with know-ledge of all languages, they composed the creed. Peter said "I believe in God the Father almighty . . . maker of heaven and earth" . . . Andrew said "and in Jesus Christ His Son . . . our only Lord" . . . James said "Who was conceived by the Holy Spirit . . . born of the Virgin Mary" . . . John said "suffered under Pontius Pilate . . . was crucified, dead, and buried" . . . Thomas said "descended to hell . . . on the third day rose again from the dead" . . . James said "ascended into heaven…sits on the right hand of God the Father almighty" …Philip said "thence He will come to judge the living and the dead" . . . Bartholomew said "I believe in the Holy Spirit" . . . Matthew said "the holy Catholic Church . . . the communion of saints" . . . Simon said "the remission of sins" . . . Thaddeus said "the resurrection of the flesh" . . . Matthias said "eternal life". (J. N. D. Kelly, *Early Christian Creeds* [New York: David McKay Co., Inc. Second Edition, 1960. Fifth Impression, 1966], p. 3.)

Obviously this is just a legend, the kind that abounded during the Middle Ages. But as with most legends, there is a grain of truth in it. The Apostles' Creed does accurately reflect the faith Jesus entrusted to His apostles. It is also true that its words and phrases were in general use even before the apostles committed the New Testament to writing and incorporated those phrases into what they wrote. Thus the apostles are in a very real sense the creed's authors.

The legend also attributes to the Apostles' Creed a direct inspiration of the Holy Spirit. Here there is another kernel of truth. Christians hold that the spoken and written words of the apostles came from the Holy Spirit. Christians also hold with St. Paul that all confession is motivated by the Holy Spirit. Thus the Apostles' Creed is inspired in a double sense. This creed is in a very real sense the teachings given the church by the Holy Spirit through the apostles, and wherever Christians throughout 18 to 19 centuries have confessed its words, there the Holy Spirit has worked faith in people's hearts. Wherever Christians confess its words we can reply with those spoken originally by Jesus to Peter: "Flesh and blood has not revealed this to you, but My Father who is in heaven" (Matt. 16:17).

The Nicene Creed

The Nicene Creed is the second most widely used confession in Christendom. In Lutheran churches it is customarily used in connection with the celebration of the Lord's Supper. This creed possesses a rarely matched majesty in language and theology. Through its words Christians share some of the most lofty thoughts composed by human beings.

The Nicene Creed was different from the other creeds that were used in the first three centuries of the church's existence. Creeds resembling the Apostles' Creed were used when a person entered the church through Baptism. The Nicene Creed came into existence expressly as a defense of the church's teaching when it was threatened by denial. Most of the Lutheran Confessions resemble the Nicene Creed in being a restatement of the truth when it was threatened.

Our confessions did not come into existence through any prescribed pattern. A confession is not produced by an arithmetical formula requiring so many bishops, so many pastors, or so many lay persons. It would be hard to demonstrate that behind any of our confessions stood anything like a committee representing a cross section of the church. No attempt was made to assure equal representation in regard to ethnic origin, race, sex, or age before a confession was formulated.

The formulating process that gave us the Nicene Creed is a good example of God's unorthodox methodology in producing confessions. Two separate and unrelated series of events converged to produce this creed. For almost 300 years after the lifetime of Jesus the Christian church and the Roman Empire were generally antagonistic towards each other. Jesus had been put to death under Roman law. As early as the seventh decade of that first century Christians were being persecuted in Rome by the mad emperor Nero. The persecution of Christians flowed and ebbed according to the whims of the local Roman officials. Many Christians in those early centuries even saw in the Roman Empire the Antichrist about whom the apostles Paul and John had spoken. The Romans had another view of the matter. They saw in Christians men who refused to assume their military obligations by serving in the army. Christians defended their refusal on the grounds that it required taking an oath to the emperor as a divine being. Worship of false gods was forbidden by the commandments of Moses, and Christians also considered such worship a denial of their faith in Jesus. Several events in the fourth century would change the standoff between the empire and the church.

Near Milan, Italy, in the year 312 a Roman general by the name of Constantine had a vision, at least according to legend, that if he replaced the Roman eagle with a Christian cross on the tops of his banners, he would be victorious in the military contest for the post of emperor. In this vision he saw a cross in the skies accompanied with the Latin inscription *In hoc signo vinces*, "In this sign you shall conquer." Constantine did conquer and became emperor of Rome. Because of the vision and his own religious commitment, he set out to Christianize the Roman Empire. This job could not be done overnight; but before another century passed, Roman citizenship also meant being "Christian." This complementary relationship between citizenship and membership in the established church still prevails in most western European countries to this day. This type of legally recognized church membership for nearly all the citizens of a nation called "Constantinian Christianity."

One of Constantine's interests for the church was its unity. His ideal of a united church as the one religion in his empire was threatened when a dissension over the Person of Jesus Christ broke out near the city of Alexandria, Egypt. A certain priest named Arius was teaching that even though the Son of God had created the world, the Son of God Himself was a creature. Arius' system was much more complex, but this denial of the eternal deity of God the Son would be most prominently associated with his name. To this day the term "Arian" is used of any person who does not accept the teaching that Jesus as God is equal and coeternal with His Father.

A long history in the church led up to this problem that crested in the early 300s with the production of the Nicene

Creed. In the years right after the ascension of Jesus into heaven, many of the early Christians sincerely believed that the Jews would recognize Jesus as the Old Testament Messiah and would serve as the vanguard in bringing the Gospel to the Gentiles. With this conviction the early Christians participated in the regular services of the temple in Jerusalem and wherever Jews gathered in their synagogs. Those Christians had a difficult time accepting the reality that most Jews would not be won for the cause of Jesus. As the first century wore on, the irreconcilable split between the synagog and the church became evident.

From this early antagonism between Christianity and Judaism, Judaism developed a monolithic concept of God as a reaction to the Christian concept of the Trinity, which was renounced as tritheism, belief in three gods. The Jewish monolithic concept of God was more than just monotheism, the belief that outside of the one true God there are no other gods. A monolithic concept of God permits no internal movement within God. Christians were naturally very sensitive to the Jewish charge of tritheism because it was tantamount to a charge of polytheism, belief in many gods, the crucial sin of the Old Testament people which led to their punishment by exile. Throughout the controversy the Christians never relinquished their belief in monotheism. For them God was one, and Jesus with the Holy Spirit shared all the divine prerogatives with the Father. But some Christians felt that compromising with certain Jewish opinions was necessary, especially if this ancient people was to be won for the Gospel.

One Christian sect, the Ebionites, with headquarters in Palestine, recognized Jesus as the fulfillment of Old Testament prophesies but held to the same kind of monolithic concept of God as did their Jewish contemporaries. For them the Father alone was God. Other Christians taught that only a divine influence had come upon Jesus. These problems remained localized and were handled without posing a threat to the entire church. The task remained to state in adequate and unequivocal terms the relationship between God, Jesus, and the Holy Spirit. Until such a statement came forth, many false and misleading opinions would be circulated as apostolic doctrine sanctioned by the church. This entire matter was not trivial, as it had to do with the understanding of God, and in any religion the concept of God is central.

In the third century, the one before Arius lived, there was an important Christian thinker by the name of Origen. He fancied himself a philosopher-theologian. Though a committed Christian, he preached the Gospel by plying his trade as a philosopher, a method not infrequently emulated since then. Too often this approach results in more changes in the Christian message than in the hearts of those who hear it. His solution to the charge of polytheism brought against Christianity was a ranking of the three Persons within God, with the Father first, the Son second, and the Holy Spirit third. This view, called subordinationism, prepared the way for Arianism. If the Son and the Holy Spirit were of inferior rank to the Father, then the next step would be their amputation from the deity. Arius was the one who wielded that ax.

Arius' ideas about God came to the attention of his superior, the bishop of Alexandria. A regional council was convoked there to condemn them. After a series of other regional councils and maneuvers in the church, some involving the Emperor Constantine himself, a more widely representative council was convened for the spring of 325 at Nicaea, a city in what is now Turkey, near Constantinople (now Istanbul), the capital of the Eastern Roman Empire.

Though Judaism offered the earliest objections to the Christian idea of God as triune, Arius' views were permeated with the transcendental view of God taken over from Greek philosophy. It was in the same intellectual climate where Origin had worked a century before. For Arius God was so perfect, so transcendental, and so removed from this world that there was no place in Him for Jesus. Of God Arius wrote: "We acknowledge one God, who is alone unbegotten, alone eternal, alone without beginning, alone true, alone possessing immortality, alone wise, alone good, alone ruler, alone judge of all."

Such a philosophically abstract concept of God did not allow for a sharing of the divine substance. God's essence was defined in such an absolute fashion that the only possible result was the radical subordination of the Son. Arius did not consider the Son eternal as the Father was. God for Arius was so absolute that He could not personally involve Himself in creation. In order to bring about the creation without affecting His absoluteness, God created the Son to serve as the creating Word. The Son or the Word was

God's creating agent, but He was not God in the absolute sense that the Father was.

These philosophically oriented views of Arius were responsible for the great religious disruption of the fourth century. Christians have always held that according to His human nature Jesus was a creature. Arius held that Jesus was a creature even according to His preexistent nature. Like all other creatures made by God, the Son or the Word was made out of nothing. He made it quite clear that the Son was in no sense coeternal with God. Yes, the Son had come into existence before matter and time, but He did *come into existence.* Arius also contended that the Son did not have the full knowledge of the Father because the Son was finite and could not grasp the infinite Father. These ideas sparked a nearly universal conflagration in the church, one that did not completely die down for centuries.

A church historian of that time reported that more than 250 bishops followed the summons of Emperor Constantine and met at Nicaea. The man having the greatest impact on the council was not a bishop but a priest serving as secretary to Alexander, the bishop of Alexandria, the diocese in which the difficulties arose. That priest's name was Athanasius. Christianity will always treasure his memory as the great defender of the Trinitarian faith.

Totally erroneous is any impression that church councils at that time were solemn, holy convocations. Hardly! Our church conventions today, which are frequently scored for a carnival and irreverent spirit, are angelic in comparison to the one held at Nicaea. The opposing parties chanted slogans against each other. Some have ironically called this the birth of hymnody!

Arius did not have a large number of sympathizers among the bishops assembled, but one segment of the council favored adopting statements which would allow for Arianism without adopting it. In the end the moderate party calling for toleration had to yield to those bishops whose views were more and more influenced by the young priest Athanasius.

In spite of the unruliness we have mentioned, the council managed to come up with these marvelous words describing Jesus:

> The only-begotten Son of God, begotten of the Father before
> all worlds, God of God, Light of Light, very God of very God,

begotten not made, being of one substance with the Father, through whom all things were made.

Each of these phrases was added by the group supporting the position of Athanasius, with the kind of perseverance used by a football team fighting for inches to make a first down in hopes of eventually getting across the goal line.

The faith of the Nicene Creed is not different from that of the Apostles' Creed, but it nails down the doctrine of Christ's deity so there can be no misunderstanding. This doctrine is confessed in several ways. The first description of Jesus, "the only begotten Son of God," is reminiscent of the Apostles' Creed. The distinctive contributions of Nicaea were the phrases "God of God, Light of Light, very God of very God, begotten, not made, being of one substance with the Father." Those phrases sound strange to us and do not make very good contemporary English. A newer translation of this creed does a better job with the phrases "God from God, Light from Light, true God from true God." The creed is saying that the Son is truly God and that His being God has been derived from the Father. The Son's deity is identical with the Father's, with whom it originated. The phrase "Light from Light" is an apt illustration. Just as a flame cannot exist without giving forth light, so the Father does not and cannot exist without giving forth the Son from His inner being. This is the meaning of the phrase "the only begotten Son of God." Just as light comes from a flame, so the Son comes from the Father. The Father is first not in point of time, but first as the eternal cause of the Son. Through this eternal action the Son is as much God as the Father.

A moderating theologian at Nicaea wanted the creed to say that Jesus was "God from true God." This the council rejected in favor of "true God from true God." The Son's deity must be expressed with the same conviction as the Father's. Through the Father's eternal act of begetting, the Son is as much God as the Father and is entitled to all honors accorded the Father.

Those who opposed Athanasius' strict views about Christ's eternal deity found they could tolerate all his phrases in the creed except one. At the phrase "being of one substance with the Father" they raised their hands in holy horror. They tried to substitute the phrase "being of like substance with the Father." The change in words from "same" to "like" (a matter one small letter in Greek) seemed insignificant, but in reality it was not. Those sympathetic to Arius raised all sorts of objections to the word "substance." This word had been used by some to mean "person" and the allies of Arius tried to accuse the group gathering around Athanasius of merging the Persons of the Father and the Son into one so that they were no longer distinct. Such was the heresy of Sabellianism, already condemned in the church. Others pointed out that the use of the word "substance" implied that the Son was made out of something like a material substance. The formulators of the creed knew of these difficulties, and for them the word "substance" in the creed means deity, what makes God "God." "Being of one substance with the Father" means that the Son is as much God as the Father is. This phrase is the real heart and core of the creed. Those who today doubt that Jesus is God still object to these phrases in the creed, especially "being of one substance with the Father."

The Son's position is so high in the divine economy that to Him is ascribed God's task of bringing creation into existence: "By whom all things were made." This was taught already by the apostle John: "Without Him was not anything made that was made" (John 1:3).

The Council of Nicaea wanted to make sure that the Arian heresy was laid to rest. It condemned the use of certain phrases which had been used by the Arians to foster their false doctrine. Among the unacceptable statements condemned by the council were: "There was a time when He did not exist"; "Before He was begotten He did not exist"; and "He was made out of nothing."

Sometimes the false impression is given that Athanasius brought peace and unity to the church through his influence on the statement adopted by the Council of Nicaea. His theological acumen was quickly recognized, and he was soon elevated to the position of bishop of Alexandria. However, the sympathizers of the Arian view caught the emperor's ear and the Arian position became dominant for a long time. Athanasius was frequently exiled from his home city. In some areas the mediating position of the Son being of *like* substance with the Father prevailed. A more radical group proclaimed that the Son was of *unlike* substance with the Father. It was one thing to adopt a position at Nicaea; it was quite another thing to see that it was upheld.

The victory of the Arian allies in the middle of the fourth

century, praise God, was not the final word. Another council met in 381 at Constantinople and with some adjustments incorporated the statement from Nicaea into what we today use as the Nicene Creed. Thus the Council of Constantinople reaffirmed the decisions made at Nicaea.

If the council of Nicaea focused on the Son, the Second Person of the Trinity, the Council of Constantinople focused on the Third Person, the Holy Spirit. The group attacking the Person of the Holy Spirit was denying His distinct personality. They did not want to be pinned down in answering the question of exactly who He is. Is He the Creator or just a creature? They remained deliberately vague. The Council of Constantinople not only reasserted the basic beliefs of Nicaea in regard to the Son, but attributed to the Holy Spirit the status of equality with the Father and the Son. This council said in 381 that He is to be worshiped and glorified together with the Father and the Son. The Holy Spirit was recognized as the Source of all life and was also confessed as the One responsible for the Holy Scriptures: "who spake by the prophets."

Because the Council of Constantinople had so much to do with formulating the Nicene Creed (especially the Third Article), some have said that for the sake of historical accuracy it should be designated the Niceno-Constantinopolitan Creed or just the Constantinopolitan Creed. But it is right that the term "Nicene Creed" should be retained, because it was at Nicaea where the church first met and conquered the Arian onslaught.

Even the Council of Constantinople did not put an end to Arianism. In the year 451 the Council of Chalcedon once more formally reaffirmed the decisions made at Nicaea and at Constantinople. Even then Arianism continued for centuries in various places until it finally spent its force.

One of the major denominational divisions still existing in the church today can be traced back to divergent views centering on the Holy Spirit's origin within the Trinity. When Christian churches whose origins are from western Europe recite the Nicene Creed they say about the Holy Spirit that He "proceedeth from the Father *and the Son*." Churches whose origins are associated with Greek Christianity omit the words "and the Son." The debate about the inclusion or exclusion of these words is called the controversy about the *Filioque*, Latin for "and the Son." The creed composed at

Constantinople in 381 and reaffirmed by Chalcedon in 451 did not state that the Holy Spirit proceeds from the Son but only that He proceeds from the Father. The wording used in our churches and others in the West comes from a later development.

This distinctive wording of the western church originates from a regional church council in Spain. Held in 589 at Toledo, its chief purpose was for a king to renounce publicly his Arian beliefs and to accept the orthodox beliefs about God according to the Nicene Creed. In his enthusiasm the king wanted to ascribe to the Son everything that was attributed to the Father. He wanted his conversion from Arianism to be complete. Thus the church's confession that the Holy Spirit proceeds from the Father should include that He proceeds from the Son. The same honor given the Father should be accorded the Son. This was the origin of the phrase about the Holy Spirit proceeding from the Father *and the Son*. Within the next 500 years this little phrase, only one word in Latin, became a theological and political football between the churches of the West, who looked to Rome for leadership, and those of the East, who looked to Constantinople. In 1054 it (among other causes) led to a split between Roman Catholicism and Eastern Orthodoxy which has never been resolved.

The Lutheran Church quite naturally retained the version which the Roman Catholic Church was using at the time of the Reformation, and thus Lutherans are accustomed to saying "who proceedeth from the Father and the Son."

The Athanasian Creed

The Athanasian Creed is generally reserved for Trinity Sunday in Lutheran churches, though at times it can be substituted for a psalm or canticle. Tucked away in the front of hymnals or prayer books, it generally escapes the notice of most of those who sit in the pew. Of all the creeds, its origins are the most hidden and mysterious. For some its theology is the most magnificent. Luther thought it was the most important theological document since the time of the apostles. When the Lutherans published their confessions in the *Book of Concord* in 1580, they included this creed right after the Apostles' and Nicene creeds. Since it predates the rise of Lutheranism and was accepted by other churches, it is classified among the catholic or ecumenical creeds.

As for its author and its exact origins, all we can do is speculate from the skimpy evidence we have at our disposal. The creed bears the name of Athanasius, the fourth-century champion of Trinitarian orthodoxy. No one will deny him the high tribute of perpetuating his memory by this creed. It is true that the Trinitarian faith of the Athanasian Creed was first put forth in its classical form by this great theologian. But he could not have been its author.

Athanasius was a thoroughly Greek-speaking theologian from Alexandria, a center renowned for Greek learning. This creed, however, was written in Latin and later had to be translated into Greek. Its theology and language reflect the situation not of the fourth century, when Athanasius lived, but of the fifth century. It may well have originated in Gaul, today's France. By the time of the reign of Charlemagne in the year 800 it was in popular use and was later to become an educational tool in the training of the clergy. But even before Charlemagne it had become a test stone of orthodoxy.

The creed has two sections, one dealing with the Trinity and the other with the doctrine of Christ. Both are unmatched in the definiteness and clarity with which they define these issues. About the Trinity this creed states that all three Persons share all the divine attributes equally. There is no trace of subordinationism. It denounces tritheism, the belief that there are three gods, with the same fervor with which it denounces Unitarianism, the belief of the Arians that God is only one Person. The distinctions among the three Persons are maintained so that there is no internal confusion within God. The second section, the one centering on Christ, reflects some of the church's thinking in the light of heresies that were encountered and answered after the time of Athanasius. Against Nestorianism, the belief that the divine and human in Jesus are separate personalities, the creed holds that Jesus is both God and man, but only one Christ, one Person. Against Eutychianism, the belief that the divine and human in Jesus are merged to form a new and mediating substance, the creed affirms that though both natures are united in one Person, they remain distinct.

Some have taken exception to the condemnatory phrases of the Athanasian Creed as offensive. But the original version of the Nicene Creed had such condemnatory phrases, as did other ancient creeds. St. Paul in New Testament times warned against those who came preaching another gospel.

Such phrases indicate the seriousness with which the early church looked upon tinkering with God's Word. The Christian church does not come condemning but bringing life. Still, the church has the obligation of clearly indicating doctrines and teachings that are not in accord with God's Word and will destroy faith.

These three creeds, the Apostles', the Nicene, and the Athanasian, are still used throughout Christendom. The words "creed" and "confession" are interchangeable. But because of their antiquity and universality the honor of the word "creed" is limited to these three ancient documents. Our next task is to see how followers of Martin Luther in the 1500s applied the truths of these creeds in their confessions. The remaining documents in the *Book of Concord* are generally referred to as the historic Lutheran Confessions. The first of these is the Augsburg Confession.

IV. Confessional Awakening at Augsburg

Soon after the controversies concerning the Person of Christ had been settled (in the 400s), the church entered the Middle Ages, the first half of which (about 500—1000) are sometimes called the Dark Ages. The Roman Empire, which had been the church's protector, gradually fell before the barbaric hordes streaming in from the north. Roman civilization, an inheritance in large part from the Greeks, was being displaced. In the 600s the new Mohammedan religion swept in from the east, inundating large areas that had once contained thriving Christian communities.

It was during those centuries, however, that much of northern Europe was Christianized. The impetus for this great task, interestingly enough, came not from the east or south but from the west. From the shores of Ireland bands of traveling monks went out with the message of the Gospel and with whatever vestiges of civilization they had managed to salvage.

During this period there was a development in the government of the church which would have far-reaching effects. In the West the decision making process gradually shifted to one man, the bishop of Rome, who became known as the pope. So gradual was the process that it went largely unnoticed. Theological responsibilities once jointly exercised by all bishops were becoming more and more concentrated in the person of the pope. Church governments became centralized in the city of Rome. In the 1500s a conflict would break out between a German monk and the bishop of Rome. The friction between these two men supplied the sparks for a confessional conflagration that spread through Europe like wildfire.

The 16th century resembles the fourth in the great number of confessional voices it produced. In fact the 16th century

44

surpasses all other centuries in the confessional concerns it both raised and answered. From it came those documents which we call our historic Lutheran Confessions. But other Christian churches in Europe were equally productive in speaking to the truth as they saw it. The churches that trace their origins to Ulrich Zwingli and John Calvin, those of the Reformed and Presbyterian tradition, have a rich confessional heritage in this period. This denominational family at this time produced the First Helvetic Confession, the Consensus Tigurinus, the Heidelberg Catechism, the Confessio Scoticana, and the Confessio Belgica. The Roman Catholic Church as it is shaped today originates from the *Canons and Decrees of the Council of Trent*, the results of an assembly that met off and on for a period of about 18 years to handle what they considered the Lutheran aberrations. Episcopalians still treasure the Third-Nine Articles and the *Book of Common Prayer*, both of which come from this same period. The 16th century provided the basic denominational structure which is still the hallmark of western Christianity.

In the forefront of the confessional vigor of the 1500s were the Lutherans, who stepped forth with the statement which is still recognized as the first and most important *Protestant* confession, the Augsburg Confession. Though it is a uniquely *Lutheran* confession, other Protestant groups respect it as the first formal declaration of what is recognized as Protestantism. Its ideas and structure have been incorporated in other confessions. To show its continued effectiveness over the past four centuries: Pope Paul VI upon the recommendation of advisers in 1976 was considering recognizing it as a valid expression of Christian truth.

On June 25, 1530, a date still honored by Lutherans, the Augsburg Confession was presented by German princes and other civil officials to Emperor Charles V. The presentation was made at a parliamentary-type gathering at Augsburg, Germany. Such meetings were called diets. This city has lent its name to the chief Lutheran confession. It may either be called the Augsburg Confession or the Augustana, the Latin for Augsburg. Some Lutheran churches and institutions incorporate Augsburg or Augustana in their official titles to indicate their allegiance to this confession and to honor those who first confessed it in that city. But this day in June 1530 was hardly the first date on which Lutherans had made confession of their faith.

Before this time Luther and his colleagues had made some great and memorable statements of their faith, all indicating the confessional vigor of the times. Luther himself started the confessional movement of the 1500s with his posting of the Ninety-Five Theses to the door of the Castle Church at Wittenberg. Though Luther would develop some of his views further after that date of Oct. 31, 1517, those theses were in every sense confessional. Protestants in general, not only Lutherans, still commemorate that date as the birthday of the Reformation.

At first Luther stood alone in making his confession known to the world. The posting of the Ninety-Five Theses was followed by a debate at Leipzig with the church scholar John Eck. At this debate Luther said that Scripture had priority over decisions of church councils in establishing doctrine, an idea incorporated in the historic Lutheran Confessions. Not much later Luther was called to appear before the emperor at Worms. When he was asked to withdraw his position, he refused. Recantation was impossible for him as he found that his ideas were drawn from the Holy Scriptures. In the 1520s others were drawn to Luther's cause. They began to be called "Lutherans" for the first time. No longer was it simply one man stating his own personal and private opinion. Rather it was a recognizable group of Christians who were offering to the world a statement of their faith, clearly drawn from the Holy Scriptures, a statement that was at many points at variance with the accepted Christianity of that day.

Before that June day at Augsburg in 1530 Lutherans participated in three meetings at which confessions, statements of their faith, were drawn up. As their ideas and even their very words were later incorporated in the Augsburg Confession, they are worth noting. In October 1529 Luther and his colleagues Philip Melanchthon, John Brenz, John Agricola, and Justus Jonas prepared the Schwabach Articles. They in turn were incorporated in the Marburg Articles, which resulted from a meeting that Luther held with his opponent Ulrich Zwingli, the Protestant reformer of the Swiss city of Zurich. These two documents provided the outline and basis for the first 21 articles of the Augsburg Confession, the ones dealing with doctrinal matters. In April 1530 Luther's prince, Elector John the Constant (brother and successor of Luther's original protector, Frederick the Wise), asked Luther and other theologians to draw up a list of churchly abuses needing correction. These were called the Torgau Articles, since they were presented to the elector at Torgau. They became the basis for the remaining seven articles of the Augsburg Confession, the ones dealing with abuses. Another confession whose ideas were taken into the Augsburg Confession was a personal one made by Martin Luther which he appended to a treatise he had written on the Lord's Supper.

At the request of Emperor Charles V representatives of the empire met at Augsburg in 1530 to resolve the religious differences that were beginning to split the empire. The Holy Roman Empire of the German Nation was a loose confederation of states, nations, cities, and principalities that maintained certain sovereign rights and often fought among themselves. It was supervised by an emperor who was elected by seven "electors" (four secular princes and three bishops), and in some vague way it was considered a continuation of the ancient Roman Empire. In accord with the ideas of those times, the emperor was also a religious figure and had to maintain both civil and religious peace and unity.

Luther, who had been granted safe conduct to a similar meeting of the empire at Worms in 1521, had now been branded a heretic by the church and an outlaw by the state. No longer was it possible for him to travel without fear of arrest or personal molestation in lands controlled by the emperor or the pope or their allies. Important as the meeting at Augsburg was, it would be impossible for him to attend. The man entrusted with representing Luther's cause and interests at Augsburg was a colleague on the theological faculty at Wittenberg, Philip Melanchthon, a scholar of ancient Greek literature who had been won for the Reformation by Luther. Luther himself during these days had traveled to Coburg Castle, a place closer than Wittenberg to the imperial proceedings. Through courier he remained in touch with the proceedings at Augsburg, which lasted for several months. On May 11 a draft of what would become the Augsburg Confession was forwarded to Luther for an opinion. His ideas formed the substance of this confession though he was not the actual author. He did not hesitate to call it his own confession.

Up to the time of the actual presentation and public

reading of the Augsburg Confession Melanchthon continually worked on it. All during the time of writing he was in contact with Elector John. Because of his stature and importance as an elector, John was the recognized political head of the Lutheran delegation at Augsburg. In June other Lutheran princes at the conclave received permission to join Elector John in presenting Melanchthon's confession as their own. No longer was the statement the confession of one church but of many. Melanchthon's introduction to the confession had to be discarded, and a new introduction was prepared by Dr. Brueck, one of the Saxon chancellors, to reflect this broader and more diversified background. The day appointed for the public reading of the document finally came. It was Saturday, June 25. The hour was three in the afternoon. The one entrusted with its reading was Dr. Christian Beyer, who also held the title of chancellor of Saxony.

Melanchthon had prepared the Augsburg Confession in Latin, the universal language of scholarship in western Europe, but a German translation by Justus Jonas was the one chosen to be read that day. This made it possible for most of the delegates to understand the confession, though it is debatable how much the Spanish-born emperor, Charles V, comprehended. It is reported that the reading of the confession made a lasting impression on those who heard it. As an act of their faith, the princes and other officials who signed the document came forward to stand before the emperor and the assembly as it was read. As long as the Lutheran Church exists their names should be remembered: Elector John, duke of Saxony; George, margrave of Saxony; Ernest, duke of Lueneburg; Philip, landgrave of Hesse; John Frederick, duke of Saxony; Francis, duke of Lueneburg; and Wolfgang, prince of Anhalt. Along with these princes, representatives from the city governments of Nuremberg and Reutlingen signed. Before the assembly at Augsburg conducted its final session, representatives from the cities of Heilbronn, Kempten, Windsheim, Weissenburg, and Frankfurt am Main also adopted this confession as their own. For all it was a courageous act of faith, as they were siding with the outlaw Luther and against their emperor and the pope.

The Augsburg Confession showed many characteristics that would become widely recognized as Lutheran. Central to it are the two chief doctrines of Lutheranism: The Scriptures as the Word of God are the source of all doctrine in the church, and justification through faith in Christ is the primary message of the Bible. In the first 21 articles are found these topics: God, Original Sin, Son of God, Justification, Ministry, New Obedience, Church, Baptism, Lord's Supper, Confession, Repentance, Use of Sacraments, Ecclesiastical Order, Ecclesiastical Usages, Civil Affairs, Christ's Return to Judgment, Free Will, Cause of Sin, Faith and Good Works, and Worship of Saints. The abuses handled in the last seven articles are the withholding of the cup from the laity in the Lord's Supper, celibacy, false ideas and practices regarding the Mass, the compulsory recital of all sins in confession, compulsory regulations concerning foods and various traditions, monastic vows, and the power of bishops.

Recent changes in the Roman Catholic Church do not make all the Lutheran objections expressed in these seven articles as pressing and as necessary as they were in 1530. Communion under both bread and wine for the laity, virtually unknown in Luther's time, is becoming more widely practiced in the Roman Catholic Church today. The Mass is now in the vernacular and no longer in Latin. The question of the celibacy of the clergy is also a subject of lively discussion in the Roman Catholic Church, though the pope still maintains that it is to be required of priests, a position no different from the one protested in the Augsburg Confession. Many of the concerns of these seven articles are still unresolved, though progress has definitely been made in others.

The most important contribution of the Augsburg Confession are the first 21 articles, dealing with doctrinal matters. They are brief, concise, and quite to the point. Though they follow along in a logical order, each forms a separate unit and can easily be understood at first reading. Not only did the Lutherans want to establish that their faith was well grounded in the Holy Scriptures, they wanted to make it clear in the minds of their opponents that they were no sect. Throughout the Augsburg Confession the Lutherans tried to show that their teachings were those of the ancient church and that in this sense they were truly catholic.

The Augsburg Confession in its structure follows a procedure used by ancient church councils. Not only is the truth clearly stated, but the false opinion that opposes this truth is explicitly rejected. In nearly all of the 21 articles, specific groups and doctrinally unacceptable opinions are singled out for condemnation. These confessors knew that the truth cannot be preserved in the church if false opinions are permitted to coexist alongside it.

The Lutherans desired to express all possible unity with their Roman Catholic opponents. They were quite willing to accept the contemporary church regulations and government if the religion itself would be reformed. This conciliatory tact and approach was not unappreciated by the Roman Catholics. They agreed to what the Lutherans had confessed about God (Article I), Christ (Article III), Baptism (Article IX), the Lord's Supper (Article X), Christ's Return to Judgment (Article XVII), and the Cause of Sin (Article XIX). In the substance of the faith, the concrete building blocks out of which the Christian faith was built, there was much agreement between the Roman Catholics and the Lutherans.

But the basic unity in the substance of the Christian religion was not matched by a similar approach to that religion. Lutherans viewed the substance of the Christian religion through their chief doctrine that a man is justified by faith without the deeds of the law. Justification understood in this way shines through all the articles and becomes part of their fabric. Melanchthon's conciliatory spirit could not cover up the Lutheran idea of justification, which crept into every corner and cranny of the confession. It was not that the Lutherans were teaching something new. They were not. But they were teaching it from a view that had lain dormant in the church for centuries, since the early postapostolic days. For almost a millennium and a half prevalent in the church was the view that works were a contributory factor to a person's salvation. The church did not deny the value of Christ's life and death. But instead of offering this Christ as total and complete salvation to the people, the church taught that Christ made it possible for people to earn salvation for themselves. To be sure, during the long centuries there were variations, but the theme of salvation through works was fundamental. As the Roman Catholic theologians read through the Augsburg Confession, they did not fail to see the Lutheran doctrine of justification surfacing throughout, even where it was present only implicitly. The Roman Catholics responded. They knew what was at stake.

The doctrine of original sin (Article II) is presented

against the backdrop of the Lutheran concept of justification. Man is described as totally depraved and alienated from God because of inborn sin. He is so inwardly corrupt towards God that any self-contribution to his own salvation is impossible from the outset. The Roman Catholic position is not explicitly but only implicitly condemned. If man was so totally corrupt as the Lutherans had stated in their confession, then man would have to rely totally on God's grace through faith without works for salvation. The Roman Catholics would not buy the Lutheran idea about original sin because it would mean a rejection of any role that man could play in his own salvation.

Striking at first sight is the brevity of the section on justification (Article IV). The major tenet of the Lutheran faith seems to deserve more than the two sentences given it by the Augsburg Confession. Equally astonishing is that the Lutherans do not even have one explicitly negative word for the Church of Rome on this subject! But a majesty of words whose meaning is unmistakably clear comes through to the reader in this solemn brevity without polemical rancor. The implications of justification can be found in the other articles, but here in Article IV its truth is presented without adornment:

> It is also taught among us that we cannot obtain forgiveness of sin and righteousness before God by our own merits, works, or satisfactions, but that we receive forgiveness of sin and become righteous before God by grace, for Christ's sake, through faith, when we believe that Christ suffered for us and that for his sake our sin is forgiven and righteousness and eternal life are given to us. For God will regard and reckon this faith as righteousness, as Paul says in Romans 3:21-26 and 4:5.

Even in an issue like the Son of God (Article III), where there was an acknowledged unity between the Roman Catholics and the Lutherans, a distinctively Lutheran view of justification can be traced in the language itself. The article uses words and phrases taken over from the Apostles' and Nicene Creeds and thus identifies itself with the church's catholic heritage. But through a few words in strategic locations Melanchthon introduces the Lutheran view of justification. Here is the key section, a recognizable combination from the two oldest creeds with my underlining of Melanchthon's *Lutheran* additions pointing to justification:

51

... there is one Christ, true God and true man, who was truly born, suffered, was crucified, died, and was buried *in order to be a sacrifice not only for original sin but also for all other sins and to propitiate God's wrath.*

If Christ's death has really accomplished these great things, the need to satisfy God's wrath through good works has disappeared. Article III is typical of the entire confession. Not only is the substantive truth of Christianity set forth in clear and also familiar language, but this truth is connected with the doctrine of the justification of the sinner before God.

In the Lutheran Church's articles of faith the two pivotal points of the Bible as the source of doctrine and the justification of the sinner through faith are always maintained. To the present this remains the hallmark of the Lutheran faith. A doctrine must be drawn from the Holy Scriptures and also find its center in Jesus Christ, who by His life and death has obtained free and full justification for the sinner. Scriptural truths are not simply set forth for their truth value in a sort of neutral way, but they are set forth to relieve sinners from sin and guilt.

The section of the Augsburg Confession dealing with prayers to the saints (Article XXI) is an example of how Lutherans relate their doctrines to the Scriptures as the source and to the justification merited by Christ and available through faith. Saints are to be remembered as examples of Christian faith. Here the Lutherans show appreciation for the church's long-standing custom of honoring the blessed dead, but they also point out in the same breath that praying to the saints for help is without Scriptural evidence. Then it points out that the Scriptures teach that we have only the promise that Christ will hear our prayers and that this type of intercession is the highest form of worship. Here we see both points: Scripture is the source of all doctrine, and all doctrine must be put in the service of sinners to free them from guilt.

What Happened to the Augsburg Confession?

Soon after its presentation to the emperor, the Augsburg Confession became recognized as the classical statement of the Lutheran faith. In 1531, one year after its presentation, Melanchthon published an edition of it in conjunction with the Apology, which we will discuss in the next chapter. These two documents, the Augsburg Confession and the Apology, both written by Melanchthon, were adopted as representative of the Lutheran position by the princes and theologians who gathered at Smalcald in 1537. The Formula of Concord, prepared in 1577, lists the Augsburg Confession as the first Lutheran statement of faith. Like all true confessions, the Augsburg Confession became a means of uniting the church on certain doctrinal points so that the truth could be distinguished from error.

One of the first controversies centering on the Augsburg Confession was resolving the question of who was its rightful possessor. This was not controversy about the ownership of the manuscripts. As these were presented to Emperor Charles V, they were placed in the imperial archives. But whose faith did the Augsburg Confesson express? Melanchthon was the author of the document, but certain German princes and city officials had subscribed it with their signatures and presented it as their faith. Melanchthon continued to think of the document as his own confession of faith. In true scholarly fashion he began publishing a series of editions to improve the original confession by polishing up the language. The changes were slight and considered insignificant and so they passed unnoticed.

In 1540, however, Melanchthon prepared an edition that could be construed as tolerating the Reformed position on the Lord's Supper. Here are the words of Article X as Melanchthon reedited them for his 1540 edition:

> Concerning the Lord's Supper, they teach that with the bread and wine Christ's body and blood are shown to those who eat the Lord's Supper.

The bread and wine are no longer explicitly called the body and blood of Christ. Neither does this statement confess that the communicants eat the body and drink the blood of Christ. It says only that the body and blood are shown to the communicants, without a word about who receives them. The Reformed position is no longer condemned as it was in the 1530 edition. Melanchthon's later editions of the Augsburg Confession were acceptable to Reformed theologians who had previously taken exception to the Lutheran position especially on the Lord's Supper. John Calvin, who was becoming the leading Reformed theologian and spokesman, could affix his signature to one of Melanchthon's later editions of the Augsburg Confession.

The 1540 edition of the Augsburg Confession became a favorite among those Lutheran theologians who secretly held a view of the Lord's Supper that was essentially Reformed. This meant that they did not have to follow Luther's view about the real presence of Christ in the bread and wine. Those adhering strictly to Luther's view on the Lord's Supper insisted on subscription to the original version of the Augsburg Confession. Adherence to this original version became the hallmark of authentic Lutheranism. It is not uncommon for churches holding to a strict Lutheran position to put the abbreviation "U.A.C." on their church cornerstones to signify their acceptance of the "Unaltered Augsburg Confession" with its clearly stated belief about the real presence of Christ in Holy Communion. In ordination rites allegiance is also made to the Unaltered Augsburg Confession.

In the year 1555 the Augsburg Confession was given a position of political importance. One of the few things in which the empire had been successful was the protection and promulgation of the Catholic faith as it was defined by the pope. Religion provided a certain amount of unity for the empire. With so much of Germany and Europe being won for the Protestant cause, the empire would have to adopt different religious goals if it was to have any meaningful existence. The dilemma was resolved by recognizing Lutheranism alongside of Roman Catholicism as being a valid religion. The ruler or ruling body of each civil unit within the empire was to determine which of the two religions was to be acceptable in his domain. The Latin phrase was "Cuius regio, eius religio"—whoever ruled determined the religion. Each principality was given the option between allegiance to the pope or the Augsburg Confession. The name given to this arrangement was the Peace of Augsburg, because it was worked out in that city. The results of this official recognition given the Augsburg Confession were both positive and negative. In a positive sense it meant that Lutheran rulers and their subjects were now able to practice their religion without any legal restraints. They would not be outlaws, as Luther had been. Privileges of the empire would not be denied them. But the Peace of Augsburg was not without its drawbacks. Many who adopted the Augsburg Confession did so because of the legal protection such subscription gave, rather than out of personal commitment or confessional loyalty.

The Augsburg Confession is still valid and important today. We should remember that 1980 will not only be the 400th anniversary of the *Book of Concord* but also the 450th anniversary of the Augsburg Confession. Both of these anniversaries could be commemorated by a careful study of this document in our churches. For instance, part of each service for a number of Sundays could be dedicated to reading through its 21 doctrinal articles.

V. The Apology—The Melanchthonian Storm

Even before the Augsburg Confession was presented, the Lutheran princes did not delude themselves into believing that the emperor or the Roman Catholic officials at Augsburg would be convinced by the arguments offered by the Lutherans. Permission to read the document before the general assembly was a major achievement. The emperor was hoping to sweep the whole Lutheran matter under the rug without their bringing a statement to the floor. On July 5, 1530, less than two weeks after the reading of the confession, the emperor announced that a committee had been formed to prepare a formal answer to it. The committee of 20 men, all solidly opposed to the Lutheran position, presented a rebuttal in 351 pages. Its extremely polemical tone and unnecessarily long length were enough for the emperor to return it to the committee for abridgement. Other drafts were drawn up, and they met the same fate at the hands of the emperor. The committee's fifth draft was found acceptable and was read on Aug. 5 to the same assembly and in the same room where the Augsburg Confession had been presented on June 25. It is called the Confutation.

The Lutherans would be entitled to a written copy of the Confutation only if they agreed to these terms: not to publish it, not to reply to it, and to accept its conclusions. Such terms, of course, were totally unacceptable. Notes had been taken during the reading of the Confutation, and more of its contents had become clearer as the Lutherans met with members of the Roman Catholic committee. Not until 1573, 43 years after the Confutation was read, were copies of it permitted to circulate, though Melanchthon claims to have seen a copy earlier.

Although no copy was made available to the Lutherans, Melanchthon had pieced its contents together well enough to begin a reply right there in Augsburg, with the imperial assembly still in session. The Lutheran princes and other civil officials serving as representatives at Augsburg did not hesitate in authorizing him to prepare an answer. In a period of three weeks Melanchthon had finished the first draft of what would become one of the historic Lutheran Confessions, called the Apology of the Augsburg Confession.

The Lutherans were given till April 15, 1531, to submit to the Confutation. Sometime in late April or early May of that year, after working on the manuscript during the intervening months, Melanchthon had completed its final edition. Later in that same year Justus Jonas prepared a German version of the Apology, working from Melanchthon's Latin text. It is not properly a translation but an expanded paraphrase, as Jonas elaborates at several points.

Melanchthon's Apology is recognized as a masterpiece of theological scholarship. Here Luther's co-worker demonstrates a full comprehension of the Holy Scriptures and the writings of the early church fathers. Lutherans have always contended that their doctrine has been taken solely from the Bible, and in the Apology Melanchthon could demonstrate how this was done. The Augsburg Confession, intended for a public reading, was too brief for doing this satisfactorily. Melanchthon also took the opportunity to present the Lutheran position as in accord with that of the fathers of the ancient church. As a classicist, he had an appreciation for the antiquities. Now he had an opportunity to put this knowledge to full use.

The Apology is different in several ways from the Augsburg Confession which it seeks to defend. It is about seven times longer. Where the Augsburg Confession frequently makes its point in just a few sentences with only a slight reference to the Bible, if at all, the Apology provides a more elaborate argumentation. Here Melanchthon provides elaborate exegesis of the Bible and a deep understanding of the church fathers. In contrast to the gentle tone of the Augsburg Confession, the polemical spirit of the Apology is striking. As we saw, at Augsburg Melanchthon had tried to side as much as possible with the Roman Catholics and against the Zwinglians and the Anabaptists. In the Apology Melanchthon's innate and usual caution is thrown to the winds. He mentions his Roman Catholic opponents by name and not merely by implication. About his authorship of the

Apology Melanchthon said: "I have entirely laid aside the mildness which I formerly exercised toward the opponents." Since the usually irenic Melanchthon seems to breathe Luther's own confessional fire into the Apology, this chapter has been called "The Apology—The Melanchthonian Storm."

Justification

The real differences between the Lutherans and the Roman Catholics became all too evident in the matter of justification, which Melanchthon treats in masterful fashion in the long Article IV of the Apology. The Catholics still asserted that works play a part in our justification. The Lutherans answered that in civil affairs man could indeed live an outwardly good life. Melanchthon could even state that Aristotle, a pagan philosopher, had written so well on ethics that no more had to be added. A respectable life is possible without divine assistance. What troubled the Lutherans about the Roman Catholic position was not man's ability to perform good works that were acceptable in the eyes of the world, but the matter of man's contributing to his own salvation. The Roman Catholics had even taught that a moral person without any knowledge of Christ could prepare for salvation by performing good works. After such an individual came to faith, he could continue to perform the same kind of good works and now earn salvation with divine aid. Melanchthon saw all this as just another form of Pelagianism, the false teaching that man earns salvation by his own works. The Lutheran position was that we are saved through faith without works. Melanchthon argued: If we are saved by works, then what use or benefit are the works accomplished by Christ? The Lutheran understanding of faith includes not only a historical knowledge, an awareness of what Christ did, but also trust, a believing acceptance that forgiveness and justification are given to all who believe. The Lutheran concept of justification is totally connected to and a natural derivative of Christ's atoning work. Since His death provides the all-sufficient propitiation and payment for sins, it cannot follow that we obtain by our works what Christ has already attained by His works. Justification for Lutherans is a confession of Christ. To teach salvation by works is a denial of Christ's vicarious satisfaction and all its benefits.

The Catholics had been willing to say that faith saves as it begins to express itself with works, but even this the Lutherans found unacceptable. Yes, faith will always express itself in works done for the neighbor, but they have no value in earning salvation. If works contributed to salvation, then man would begin to put his trust in his works and not in Christ. Christ and what He has accomplished must remain at the center of the Christian religion.

Since the Apology is a defense of the Augsburg Confession against the arguments of the Roman Catholic party in the Confutation, the outline for both Lutheran documents is the same. The material in the Augsburg Confession to which the Roman Catholics objected is repeated with greater elaboration.

The Apology was soon accepted as a confessional document along with the Augsburg Confession. When Luther's colleagues met to work out an agreement with the Protestant theologians from southern Germany in 1536 at Wittenberg, the Apology was included along with the Augsburg Confession as a document to which all the participants subscribed. At a very important meeting at Smalcald in 1537, about which more will be said in the next two chapters, the same subscription to the Apology took place. Still again in the last of the historic Lutheran Confessions, the Formula of Concord, it is given confessional status with this glowing tribute:

> We therefore unanimously pledge our adherence to this Apology also, because in it the cited Augsburg Confession is clearly expounded and defended against errors and also because it is supported with clear and irrefutable testimonies from the Holy Scriptures.

VI. Smalcald—Getting Ready For the Battle Never Fought

At the time of the presentation of the Augsburg Confession Luther's followers wanted to be understood as a group within the total church structure looking for a redress of grievances. Although even then it was doubtful whether a real reconciliation was possible, still the attempt was made and the integrity of the emperor and the princes was beyond reproach in their sincere desire to rectify the situation. Charles V had sufficient honor to let the Lutherans make a public profession of their faith. But even before the meeting at Augsburg was over, the deep chasm between the Lutherans and the Roman Catholics broke through the false calm at the surface. Subsequent events following Augsburg would make public the permanent split between the two groups. The rapid and not overly careful response of the Roman Catholics in the Confutation not only indicated that they were not going to change their stance but that they were not going to pay much attention to the Lutheran position. Melanchthon's publication of the Apology of the Augsburg Confession showed that the Lutherans were not going to back down.

The irreconcilable differences between the two churches had grave consequences for the empire. The rulers of nations in those days took their responsibility to the church very seriously. For instance, Christopher Columbus' expedition in 1492 was undertaken with the understanding that the Catholic faith would be spread among the inhabitants of the lands he discovered. This was part of the charter agreement between him and Queen Isabella of Spain when she outfitted the ships. Her grandson and successor on the Spanish throne,

Charles V, now also the elected head of the Holy Roman Empire, felt this obligation to the Catholic faith just as strongly. He now adopted the solution of calling a council, for which the Lutherans had long asked. He met with Pope Clement VII in Bologna to discuss the convening of a widely representative church council. The next year the pope sent an emissary to Germany with a promise that a council would be conducted. Clement VII was succeeded by Paul III. After several years the new pope issued a bull, *Ad dominici gregis,* which set May 23, 1537, as the date for the convening of a council at Mantua, an imperial city on the Italian side of the Alps. The popes and Charles V were throughout the years military enemies and distrusted each other. Mantua belonged to the emperor, but with its location on the southern side of the Alps the pope would have a definite military advantage in any possible conflict. Another bull issued by the pope precluded any possibility for an open and free council. The stated purpose of the council was "the utter extirpation of the poisonous, pestilential Lutheran heresy." Such language is hardly an invitation to open discussion.

Upon receiving this kind of invitation, the Lutherans were divided among themselves about the wisdom of accepting it. Luther was immediately in favor of attending this council. The pope's blasts had never deterred him. Luther's enthusiasm for going to Mantua was not shared by all, however, especially the princes. As governmental leaders they were aware of the political manipulations of pope and emperor. The Lutherans had to resolve the differences among themselves before responding to the invitation. Unlike the ancient church councils, where the bishops participated as equals, the council at Mantua would be controlled by the pope. Its results were determined by him before its first session met. Could the Lutherans participate in a meeting if its purpose was to eradicate their beliefs?

Elector John of Saxony, Luther's own prince, accepted the invitation under protest. The Lutheran reply objected to any council prejudiced by the pope and not general, free, and impartial. After the response was sent off, the elector requested Luther to prepare a statement setting forth the essentials of the Lutheran faith. It was to state doctrinal limitations beyond which the Lutherans would not go. The result of this request is what we know today as the Smalcald Articles, a part of our *Book of Concord.* Points which

Melanchthon glossed over in the Augsburg Confession are tackled head on by Luther in these articles. He had reached the point where, confronted by the pope, he would give up nothing.

Luther was given this assignment by the elector on Aug. 20, 1536, but it was not until December of the same year that he began and finished the work. After revisions and some editing were offered by his colleagues, the articles were presented to the elector on Jan. 3, 1537. The document's ultimate destination was a joint gathering of Lutheran theologians and princes scheduled for the German city of Smalcald on Feb. 8, 1537. Each of the groups were to meet separately. The theologians would concentrate on the doctrinal points to be discussed at the council called by the pope. The princes in a separate session would discuss its political ramifications. Luther, who had become ill in December while working on the articles, became ill again and could not attend the meeting. Though this document would bear the name "Smalcald Articles," they were never put on the agenda of a plenary session of both the theologians and princes at the conference. Melanchthon was pushing for the adoption of the Augsburg Confession and another document, the Wittenberg Concord, as the basis for stating the Lutheran position. The year before (1536) Luther and the south German theologians had adopted the Wittenberg Concord, which did not seem as strong as it could have been on the matter of the Real Presence in the Lord's Supper. For the ever compromising Melanchthon, Luther's articles prepared for Smalcald were just too strong, and he succeeded in keeping them from coming up for debate. Thus they were never formally adopted.

All of the maneuverings at Smalcald proved to be academic, as the princes finally decided to decline the invitation to the pope's council at Mantua. But Melanchthon was not totally successful in scuttling Luther's articles. After the assembly had officially adjourned, 44 of the 49 in attendance remained there to affix their signatures to Luther's articles. Melanchthon, too, signed the Smalcald Articles, but with an interesting condition. He wrote that he would acknowledge the pope's supremacy in the church if the pope would allow the preaching of the Gospel and would admit that he held his position by human rather than divine right. The pope and Roman Catholic theologians have never given Melanchthon's idea any serious consideration. With a supremacy only of human and not of divine right the pope would become just another bishop.

When Melanchthon's doctrinal meanderings became noticeable, especially after Luther's death, the Smalcald Articles were recognized as the expression of authentic Lutheranism. The Formula of Concord says that they are a correct interpretation of the Augsburg Confession. In the Small Catechism Luther is the teacher and in the Large Catechism Luther is the preacher, but in the Smalcald Articles Luther is the confessor. In this document he squarely attacks the Roman Catholic Church in such matters as the Mass, monasteries, invocation of saints, and the papacy itself. Even some Lutherans would rather forget that in these articles Luther in no uncertain words brands the pope as the Antichrist.

Luther's judgment on the pope is frequently ignored as a discourteous remark or dismissed as an ecumenical embarrassment. But what Luther was saying here should be given some attention. First of all he was in no way casting a judgment against the Christians within the Roman Catholic Church. Luther had contended that Christ's church is found wherever the Gospel is preached, and this certainly includes the Roman Catholic Church. Nor was Luther making a judgment about the personal salvation of any individual. This is God's prerogative alone. His judgment against the papacy as Antichrist was against that office or any institution which in God's name teaches doctrines contrary to what God has commanded. Luther saw the concept of being Antichrist as related to justification by faith. As long as the pope continues to endorse the doctrine that men can earn their salvation through works, regardless of which works he designates, he remains the Antichrist. But the verdict does not have to limited to the pope. It can be rendered against any Christian church leader who in God's name makes requirements for salvation which God Himself does not require. Quite specifically it applies to official church teachers who proclaim works and not faith as the way to heaven and salvation. Some claim that the modern papacy has backed away from the severe position which Luther with equal severity attacked. The papacy does seem to make exceptions for those who do not recognize its authority, but Lutherans object to the whole idea that the papacy should have the authority to make such decisions.

Luther's Smalcald Articles are not patterned after the Augsburg Confession with its orderly and concise parts. After a personal introduction describing his and the church's situation, Luther divides this confession into three parts. Part I is a brief restatement of the Trinitarian faith with sentences taken over from the Apostles' Creed. Part II has four articles, in which Luther directly singles out what he finds most objectionable in the Roman Catholic Church. He calls the Mass "the greatest and most horrible abomination," as it contradicts the fundamental article of justification by faith alone. Luther says that the church could exist very well without the papacy. His attack on the opulence of the Church of Rome is picturesque. But his main argument is that its doctrines and practices are destructive of the chief article of justification by faith. Fifteen short articles comprise the third part. Most of this material is discussed in the Augsburg Confession and the Apology. In Luther's treatment there is no doubt that the differences between him and the Roman Catholics are significant. In Part III, Article VI, "The Sacrament of the Altar," Luther distinguishes his position from both the Reformed and the Roman Catholic. The Reformed would find it impossible to subscribe to Luther's position on the Lord's Supper as "the true body and blood of Christ and that these are given and received not only by godly but also by wicked" men. On the other hand he calls transubstantiation a "subtle sophistry."

Those who want to recapture the vital confessional spirit of Luther—a confidence so grounded in God through the Holy Scriptures that it could defy pope and emperor—can find it in the blunt and vibrant language of the Smalcald Articles.

VII. Other Business at Smalcald—Melanchthon's Treatise on the Power and Primacy of the Pope

Since Philip Melanchthon's Treatise on the Power and Primacy of the Pope originated at Smalcald and was there officially adopted, it was later appended to Luther's Smalcald Articles and erroneously considered part of that document. The Formula of Concord, for instance, says that the Treatise "constitutes an appendix to the Smalcald Articles." Actually they are two separate documents.

The years following the presentation of the Augsburg Confession not only brought dilemmas to the emperor, who had to solve the problem of having non-Catholic officials in his realm, but it brought problems to the Lutherans, who had to provide church organizations for their realms. The medieval church organization knew only of the pope appointing bishops, in consultation with the local ruler, the bishops then appointing priests. The process of selection varied somewhat from land to land, but for each country there was a set procedure. Everyone was so used to this system that after centuries of a church controlled by the pope it was hard for people and clergy to think of the church without him.

The pope's invitation to a council at Mantua helped many Lutherans think through the matter of his place in the church. A pope who had convened a council for his own purposes, with ready-made decisions and with the demand that Lutheranism be annihilated, really had no right to be head of the church. The rejection of the pope's claims was eloquently expressed in the princes' rejection of his invitation to the council at Mantua. The Lutherans were saying loud and clear that they were going to have a church without the pope.

Now the Lutherans were faced with the problem of offering a statement defining and defending their separate status as a church body autonomous from Rome. Melanchthon's Treatise describes the independence of the Lutheran churches from papal power and shows how they can continue to operate without the supervision of the pope's bishops.

Perhaps independence from the pope's control should have been proclaimed at Augsburg in 1530. There the Lutherans had for their audience the emperor and the pope's representatives. But as we have seen, Melanchthon at Augsburg was hoping and working for reconciliation. A statement of independence would hardly have served that purpose. Now nearly seven more years had elapsed, and it was time to state clearly the Lutheran position in regard to the papacy.

In the Smalcald Articles Luther had set the tone for the Lutheran antagonism against the pope, but it was left to Melanchthon to set forth with care the specific reasons for the Lutheran objections. This treatise has two parts, one dealing with the pope and the other with bishops. In the section on the pope, Melanchthon tackles his claim to absolute supremacy in church and state. Lutherans and Roman Catholics would not quarrel about Christ's lordship, but Lutherans would not agree that this lordship should be excercised through the pope. The pope's claims were summarized in three points: 1. The pope is the supreme head of the church by divine right; 2. the pope not only supervises the church on earth, but he is the head of all earthly rule; 3. submission to the pope is necessary for salvation. The Lutherans saw all these claims as destructive of the central doctrine of justification by faith.

In regard to the first claim, the pope's supremacy over the church, Melanchthon shows from Scripture that the apostles' authority was derived from Christ and not from Peter, whom the Roman Catholic party regarded as the first pope. Then Melanchthon brings in examples from early church history. He shows that the pope or the bishop of Rome, his first title, was not regarded as supreme in the early church and that even after he attached a certain kind of importance to himself, his opinions and directives were frequently ignored. Melanchthon also found objectionable the pope's claim to rule all earthly kingdoms with threats of excommunication on those who refused political submission to him. Lutherans have always maintained God's separate rule in church and state and deny all political power or authority to the church. But worst of all was the pope's assertion that outside of him there was no salvation. This claim put him in direct conflict with the doctrine of justification by faith in Christ alone. Even the usually irenic and conciliatory Melanchthon had to say in the Treatise that the papacy had all the marks of the Antichrist.

The second part of the Treatise is a self-contained unit and is entitled "The Power and Jurisdiction of Bishops." It speaks of the right of churches to ordain pastors when the regularly appointed bishops refuse to provide them for the congregations. With the coming of the Lutheran Reformation, most of the bishops remained loyal to the pope, who had appointed them. Many of these bishops were prince-bishops and ruled their provinces as secular rulers. They had a double loyalty to the pope and emperor, and following Luther would have meant forfeiting privileges in church and empire. The bishops who remained loyal to the pope refused to provide pastors for the churches in their jurisdiction which had been won for the cause of Lutheranism. Outside of Germany some bishops were won for Lutheranism, and in those cases the church administration supervised by bishops went on unhindered and in the usually prescribed way. Bishops continued to ordain and appoint pastors for the people. This happened, for example, in Sweden, where the churches are still supervised by bishops whose ordinations go back in an unbroken line to pre-Reformation times (the so-called "apostolic succession"). But what about those areas where the bishops were not won for Lutheranism? Where would these people get pastors? The overwhelming majority of Lutherans found themselves in this situation. Melanchthon's Treatise provides the answer.

The Lutheran answer in "The Power and Jurisdiction of Bishops" is that the churches retain the right to elect and ordain pastors when the regularly appointed bishops refuse to do so. Also asserted is the divine validity of an ordination performed by a pastor who is not a bishop, when the regular bishop refuses to do so. Melanchthon asserts that all who preside over the churches, whether they are designated as pastors, elders, or bishops, have the power to ordain. By custom and tradition the bishops began to excercise this right exclusively; but where the bishops arbitrarily refuse to provide pastors, the churches retain this right.

When the Lutherans adopted Melanchthon's Treatise, they had in effect already moved out from under the pope's control and had rejected his teachings. Luther and his colleages were already preparing theological students at Wittenberg and were ordaining them. Melanchthon's Treatise explains something that had already happened, and it defends the validity of the Lutheran ministry even where bishops do not cooperate in ordaining pastors.

VIII. The Pastoral Heart— Luther's Two Catechisms

From the very beginning Luther was interested in making sure that the laity and not just the clergy would be aware of the great principles of the Reformation. The Reformation had begun in a university and among the clergy, but its principles centered around lay participation in the theological task. Ultimately all doctrine was for the people, who had the task and obligation to test it on the basis of the Scriptures. The church consisted of all baptized Christians and not just the hierarchy. If the people were going to judge doctrine, they would need a Bible in their own language. This drove Luther to translate first the New Testament and then the Old Testament in record-breaking time—a magnificent feat for one man, but even more astonishing when Luther's other accomplishments and responsibilities are considered.

Throughout his life Luther remained at his post as a professor of theology at the University of Wittenberg. But his existence was not that of an isolated academician. Luther was always busy lecturing to students and preaching in church. His transcribed sermons fill volumes. The local pastor, Bugenhagen, a personal friend of Luther's and one of his chief troubleshooters, would frequently be away from his pulpit to do tasks in other parts of Germany and Europe. During these long periods of absence Luther occupied the pulpit and assumed the other pastoral functions. Luther never had an official call as a pastor to a congregation, but he was a pastor in a very real sense.

The Ninety-Five Theses, which began the Reformation, were written in Latin, not the language of the people, but it was for the plight of the people that they were written. Luther saw the people buying forgiveness of sins with money, and his pastoral heart was moved to post those theses on the door of the Castle Church in Wittenberg on Oct. 31, 1517. His concern for the people remained with him the rest of his life.

The nearly universal spiritual ignorance among both clergy and people demanded a program of religious education for all. The blame for this ignorance rested squarely on the priests, some of whom could barely recite the Lord's Prayer and the Apostles' Creed. Many recited the Mass in Latin but had little idea of what they were saying. Trips conducted throughout the churches of Saxony only impressed on Luther and his colleagues that immediate action would have to be taken. Luther's two catechisms are directed to this bleak situation.

Nearly all church members are familiar with the term "catechism" as a book used in preparing persons for church membership through Baptism or preparing children for fuller participation in the church's life through confirmation. Catechisms were not Luther's invention; they had been used for a long time.

Lutherans do not need an introduction to Luther's Small Catechism. It remains the standard text for confirmation classes. Luther wrote another document, the Large Catechism, which is not so widely known. Both these catechisms are part of our historic Lutheran Confessions. Both date from 1529, with the Large Catechism reaching the press first. The Large Catechism is the result of Luther's own reediting of sermons he delivered between December 1528 and March 1529 and follows the outline so familiar to Lutherans in the Small Catechism—Ten Commandments, Apostles' Creed, Lord's Prayer, Baptism, and the Lord's Supper. Luther had deliberate purpose in the organization of his catechisms. The commandments showed man his need; the creed showed him where help was to be found; and the Lord's Prayer showed him how he could ask and then receive the help he needed.

Luther never tired of saying that he remained a student of the catechism all his life. By this he meant that the Ten Commandments, the Apostles' Creed, and the Lord's Prayer had depths which he had never plumbed.

Luther intended that the Large Catechism be used chiefly as sermon material by the clergy. The pastors and priests at that time were burdened by two prominent weaknesses:

preaching and theological knowledge. They were not used to preaching. Most of their attention had been focused on the mechanics of the Mass. Even the priests sympathetic to Luther's Reformation lacked a full comprehension of evangelical doctrine. Luther's Reformation was destined to move ahead on the principle that the Biblical doctrine was to be publicly proclaimed to the people. The Large Catechism was to make this possible by providing sermon material that priests not accustomed to public proclamation and unsure of evangelical doctrine could conveniently and safely use. It was in all senses a very practical document, immediately usable, which fostered the essential Reformation principles.

From the pages of the Large Catechism the reader sees Luther in his double role as preacher and reformer. Here is the voice of the man who has come to the personal conviction that justification is by faith alone, and now that voice speaks with prophetic assurance. A certain unevenness among its sections reflects the ruddy jaggedness of Luther's confessional personality.

If we had to pick out a section characteristic of Luther, it would be his explanation of the First Commandment, "You shall have no other gods." He he launches into a discussion not of the polytheism of pagans in faraway lands but of the personal idolatry of which even Christians are capable. This he connects with faith, trust, and justification. Luther writes: "To have a god is nothing else than to trust and believe him with our whole heart." All men, according to Luther, are religious; the objects of their devotion become their gods. Luther's censure of idolatry is directed against those who put their trust in anything or anyone besides the God who has given up His Son for us. Preachers who regularly read the Large Catechism will learn to speak directly to the people as Luther did. He was not only a great theologian, but he was a preacher who could speak to the common man on his own terms.

The Large Catechism has five parts, but the section on the Commandments fills up nearly half the space. The section on the Apostles' Creed is surprisingly short by comparison. Luther does not address Himself to the doctrinal intricacies of the inter-Personal Trinitarian relationship but speaks of the Father as Creator, the Son as Redeemer, and the Holy Spirit as the One who dispenses Christ's gifts to the church.

The Lord's Prayer gives Luther another opportunity to

show the importance of honoring God by hearing and doing His Word. The evil that persists in afflicting the Christian is not an impersonal force but Satan Himself. "Deliver us from evil," the prayer's final petition, is man's plea to God to rescue him from Satan, the worst of all foes.

Baptism, the fourth section of the Large Catechism, shows in what high regard Luther held this sacrament. For him Baptism was valid because God had commanded it, and not even the unbelief of the one who received Baptism could annul it. Luther strongly opposed the Anabaptists, who were insisting that those baptized as infants had to rebaptized. He saw Baptism as offering God's grace. To despise Baptism, including infant Baptism, was to despise the God who had instituted it. Baptism without faith was still valid as God's act, but Luther never surrendered his doctrine that even children at the time of their Baptism can believe.

In his discussion of the Lord's Supper, Luther emphasized that the Sacrament is God's work and not man's. He also stressed that in it we obtain forgiveness of sins, as well as strength and refreshment, and that we must receive the Sacrament in faith.

Luther's Large Catechism, which appeared in 1529, did not gain official confessional recognition till after his death, though it was widely used. The Formula of Concord mentions it as a document to which Lutherans adhere. From the viewpoint of·the date of its writing, it is the oldest of the specifically Lutheran confessions, a year older than the Augsburg Confession.

Luther's Small Catechism is an overwhelmingly blessed result of his concern that the people be instructed in the principles of the Reformation. The influence of this small pamphlet-sized document has been vast. For 450 years children preparing for their first reception of the Lord's Supper have read, studied, and memorized Luther's words, and old people recalling its beautiful phrases have died with its comfort on their lips.

Of both catechisms the Formula of Concord says: "They are 'the laymen's Bible' and contain everything which Holy Scripture discusses at greater length and which a Christian must know for his salvation." This is no exaggeration! There is no doctrine which is not taught here, and every false doctrine contradicts its principles.

While Luther was preparing the Large Catechism, he undertook the writing of the Small Catechism. Several years before, Luther had urged the task of preparing this kind of catechism on his colleagues, but when they failed to produce anything, he undertook the task himself. Generally the Small Catechism is regarded as something for children, but in Luther's title it is obvious that he intended it first "for pastors and preachers." The preface indicates that they were to use the catechism in the training of the youth after they had first understood it themselves. Soon it became a household item in many families in the Reformation countries, a staple in the devotional life of the people. To this day it remains a classical and usable expression of the Christian faith.

The Small Catechism underwent several revisions by Luther himself. The version adopted into the *Book of Concord* has nine parts: I. The Ten Commandments; II. The Creed; III. The Lord's Prayer; IV. The Sacrament of Holy Baptism; V. Confession and Absolution; VI. The Sacrament of the Altar; VII. Morning and Evening Prayers; VIII. Grace at Table; IX. Table of Duties. Its brevity, simplicity, clarity, and winsome approach give this document true theological greatness, putting it in a class with the Apostles' and Nicene Creeds.

Those brought up in the Lutheran Church were introduced to the Small Catechism by becoming acquainted with Luther's explanations of the Ten Commandments. Few Lutherans appreciate the theological greatness of these explanations. The commandments themselves are taken from the Old Testament books of Exodus and Deuteronomy. These commandments given through Moses are mostly negative. The words "Thou shalt not" are their hallmark. In his explanations Luther adds a positive aspect to them and makes this the most important. Behind Luther's plan there is a significant theological reason. As long as man is outside of God's grace, he hears God's law as one loud "No," telling him to stay away from forbidden things. Through faith in Jesus Christ the believer is now in a new relationship with God and begins to understand the Law as something good and positive, something that describes his relationship to a loving Father. The commandment "You shall not kill" provides an example of Luther's principle. Not only are we to avoid injuring our neighbor in any way but are to come to his aid in danger. Each commandment serves its ultimate function not when it cordons off a prohibited part of man's life but when it provides positive instruction for his whole existence.

In Luther's explanation of the First Commandment the

Law statement with a prohibition "You shall have no other gods" becomes a statement of faith and justification, "We should fear, love, and trust in God above all things." Here is an invitation to put our total reliance on God. Luther's Small Catechism is not for unbelievers, but for those who fit under the category of the First Commandment's explanation of fearing, loving, and trusting in God. Trust would be the best synonym for Luther's concept of faith.

Also basic to Luther's approach in the Small Catechism is his dependence on the Holy Scriptures. In explaining the Sabbath regulations in the Third Commandment, he warns against despising God's Word and urges attentive listening to its preaching. His explanations of the sacraments also demonstrate his reliance on the principles of justification and Scripture as the only authority. Both Baptism and the Lord's Supper offer forgiveness of sins. The reason for such trust in what these sacraments offer comes from the Scriptures' description of them. For Luther all theology served justification, but equally true for him was that theology had to be drawn from Scripture as the Word of God.

Luther's explanation of the Apostles' Creed must certainly belong to the greatest literature of all time, both for its theological greatness and its beauty of expression. He has an individual explanation for each of the creed's three sections. He focuses the work of each of the three divine Persons on the believer in an individual way. Thus the God who created heaven and earth must be understood as the God responsible for my existence. Luther's explanation of the creed's Second Article has been learned and memorized by so many that is has become a classic expression of the Christian faith. Here is not just another recitation of the historical facts of the life of Jesus, but a stirring confession that the One who is true God and true man "is my Lord, who has redeemed me, a lost and condemned creature." Luther goes right to the heart of the Atonement by saying that Christ has purchased the believer with His holy, precious blood. He saw Christ and His work all focused on the believer's personal salvation. This is the thought he grasped in the explanation of the creed's Second Article. For these words alone, Luther's memory deserves cherishing.

Frequently overlooked is that Luther retained the personal or private confession of sins to the pastor. Both catechisms contain instructions on how this should be done.

Many Protestants cringe at the idea of sharing their private and secret thoughts with someone else. Luther gave specific advice on making this kind of personal confession. He did not see confession as an unbaring of the naked soul by listing in graphic detail the specifics of personal transgressions. He saw sin as the failure to perform the duties assigned to each person. This failure was the sin to be confessed.

Luther's concept of confession was directly tied to his view of good works. In the Roman Catholic Church a really *good* work was doing something *religious,* like taking a pilgrimage, fasting, or paying for the recitation of a Mass. For Luther—and this is one of his greatest insights—a good work is performing those functions in life which are demanded by one's calling or occupation. Luther in his "Table of Duties," a part of the catechism, saw good works as staying right at the place and occupation where God has placed one. Sin becomes the failure to carry through these obligations faithfully. Thus confession before the pastor means that employers, employees, parents, and children examine themselves on the basis of their particular calling or responsibility.

By the way, many feel that the disuse of confession in the sense that Luther understood it has been a great loss to Lutheranism.

The Small and Large Catechisms received official recognition in 1577 by the Formula of Concord and were incorporated in the 1580 *Book of Concord.* By that time they had already been in use for half a century. To this day the Small Catechism remains an outstanding standard and symbol of confessional Lutheranism. For 450 years it has shaped Lutheran theology, thought, and expression.

IX. Getting the Log out of Your Own Eye— The Formula of Concord

When Martin Luther died on Feb. 18, 1546, Lutheranism was already an established religious force. It had all happened in less than 30 years. On Oct. 31, 1517, an unknown monk had asked for discussion on several theological points. Now the thoughts of this man had become the faith for large segments of the world's population. At the time of his death all the documents we recognize as historic Lutheran Confessions, with the exception of the Formula of Concord and the Introduction to the *Book of Concord,* had been written.

Luther was not unaware of the effect of his theology. He also knew that after his death the church associated with his name would suffer grave calamities. One did not need the gift of divine prophecy to make such predictions. Any movement founded on the ideas of a man and nourished by him for over a generation is going to suffer a shock when it loses the benefit of his personal guidance. Luther knew of the aberrations and difficulties that some of his colleagues entertained. But so forceful was his personality that he successfully restrained them.

Luther's fears proved to be well-founded. Some of the views held by his colleagues at the University of Wittenberg were serious errors. Political problems in the empire compounded the difficulties. The emperor continued to press for the idea of one united church under the pope and was determined to use all military force at his disposal to achieve that goal.

The story of this chapter is one of death and rebirth. It is the account of how confessional Lutheranism barely survived and how it then reblossomed with renewed vigor. The

76

first 30 years of Lutheranism (1517—46) are the history of Lutheran survival in the face of threats from Roman Catholicism and then Reformed theology. The Lutherans were tempted either to go back to Rome or to go forward to join Zwingli, Calvin, and the Reformed. The second 30 years (1546—77) are the history of how Lutheranism managed to survive in the face of dissensions. Perhaps the threats of the second 30 years were more serious because now the enemies of Lutheranism called themselves "Lutheran" too. After this second struggle there was a restatement of Luther's faith in the Formula of Concord, a document reflecting the struggles among the Lutherans themselves. Its publication was accompanied by a reprinting of all those documents which we know as the historic Lutheran Confessions. After this there was to be no doubt about what it meant to be Lutheran. It meant accepting the Formula of Concord and the other Confessions listed there. This chapter is dubbed "Getting the Log out of Your Own Eye" because, unlike the earlier Lutheran Confessions, the Formula of Concord speaks primarily and mostly to internal Lutheran problems and only secondarily to the false opinions of the Roman Catholics, the Reformed, the Anabaptists, and others.

The importance of the Formula of Concord can better be appreciated if we understand what happened between the death of Luther in 1546 and the adoption of the Formula in 1577. During this 30-year span Lutheranism suffered at the hands of both deceitful theologians and princes bent on political intrigue to improve their lot.

Luther died on Feb. 18, 1546, and by June 26 of that same year the emperor and the pope overcame their long-standing animosity and entered into an alliance whose purpose was to reimpose Roman Catholicism through military force.

The Lutheran princes had already established their own defensive alliance, the Smalcald League, formed in connection with the meeting discussed in chapters VI and VII. During Luther's lifetime the emperor could not act against Luther because of internal dissension in his empire, but now the emperor's old enemies became allies or had been neutralized. Henry VIII, king of England, who once thought of aligning himself with the Protestant princes by marrying Anne of Cleves, had joined the nephew of his first wife and his former enemy, the emperor and king of Spain, Charles V, into forcing France into an alliance. Charles could not move effectively against the Lutherans if his western flank was open to an attack from the French. The English took care of that problem. The troubles on the southeastern frontier of the empire were dissipated as the Turks became concerned with problems in Persia. The emperor had established congenial relations with Rome. The pope acceded to the emperor's wish for a council, which was eventually held in Trent between the years 1545 and 1563. From this council would come the classical expression of Roman Catholicism which has remained determinative till Vatican II in our time. With his armies and council the emperor was bent on achieving unity in state and church within the imperial boundaries. If all worked well, the dream of one Holy Roman Empire of the German Nation would be fulfilled. To achieve this goal the Smalcald League would have to be dismembered. And it was.

From the Lutheran side there were defections to the imperial cause. The emperor offered Maurice, the head of ducal Saxony, the title of Elector of Saxony, which included the lands belonging to electoral Saxony, if he would help him supress the Smalcald League. The temptation was too great for Maurice to resist. Another prominent Lutheran prince, Philip of Hesse, had broken imperial law by committing bigamy. The emperor promised him exemption from punishment if he deserted the Lutheran cause. Philip accepted the offer but still was imprisoned when the emperor failed to keep his promise.

Having ruined the Smalcald League, the emperor easily defeated the Lutherans at Muehlberg on the Elbe River, on April 24, 1547. These were some of the saddest and most tragic days for Lutheranism. Our sympathy is directed specifically to Elector John Frederick the Magnanimous, the son and successor of John the Constant. He had held the Lutheran cause together at Smalcald in 1537. Now he was defeated and imprisoned by the emperor. The memory of this dear prince shall remain a treasure to all confessional Lutherans. Prison did not daunt his spirit, but he confessed his Lutheranism even more boldly. For him the worst penalty was being deprived in prison of Luther's writings, from which he took consolation.

With his victories over the Lutheran territories safely behind him, the emperor began quickly to reintroduce Roman Catholic doctrine and customs into the churches of the Reformation. The document bringing about these changes was called the "Augsburg Interim," published in 1548. The term "Interim" designated a temporary solution until the council called by the pope could provide a more permanent one. So severe was the Augsburg Interim that Maurice, the new elector of Saxony, issued the milder Leipzig Interim in the same year. The Lutherans' chief objection to the Leipzig Interim was the reintroduction of certain Roman Catholic customs and practices as mandatory. For more on this whole matter, see pages 155 ff.

As quickly as the fortunes of the Lutheran princes, lands, and churches had declined, they were revived when the emperor's forces no longer menaced them. Maurice, the new elector of Saxony, considered a turncoat by many of the Lutherans, had a change of heart. Public opinion was turning against him, so in 1552 he attacked the emperor and conquered his forces stationed in the Austrian city of Innsbruck. Overnight the ally of the pope became the "Champion of Protestantism," and he was hailed by this title as he entered the imperial city of Augsburg. With Protestant forces in control of much of Germany, the Lutherans could exact more favorable terms from the emperor. A treaty signed at Augsburg in 1555 ushered in an era of political peace in the Lutheran lands, for the Peace of Augsburg, as the documnet was officialy called, gave them legal recognition in the empire.

The restoration of political peace in the Lutheran lands was not accompanied by theological harmony and concord in the churches, however. Three different factions developed among the Lutherans. One was headed by Melanchthon, who was generally recognized as Luther's natural successor. Called Philippists, after Philip Melanchthon, this group favored some types of reconciliation with the Reformed and the Roman Catholics. They permitted the reintroduction of Roman Catholic customs into their churches without too much objection. These men were chiefly associated with the University of Wittenberg, where Luther had taught for so many years. At the opposite end of the spectrum were the so-called "Gnesio-Lutherans" ("genuine Lutherans"), led by a young theologian named Matthias Flacius. They advocated an uncompromising adherence to Luther's views and demanded exposure of Melanchthon's group as being un-Lutheran. The last group to emerge, occupying a center position, was completely committed to Luther's views but saw the restoration of harmony among the Lutherans at their first goal. From this third group emerged the Formula of Concord. It spoke directly to the problems which had caused internal strife, but it spoke in such a way that unity could be restored.

Volumes have been written about the origin of the Formula of Concord; we can only touch on a few highlights. Johann Brenz stated the distinct position of Lutheranism over against Calvinism. He died in 1570, seven years before the Formula was written, but he is considered one of its fathers. Brenz's work was continued by Jakob Andreae, the author of a document published in 1567 singling out the points of controversy among the Lutherans. He also published a series of sermons in 1573 which in simple language pointed out how the troublesome controversies could be settled. At the suggestion of the prominent theologian Martin Chemnitz (often called "the second Martin," thus making him comparable to Luther) and others, Andreae reedited his sermons into a document called the Swabian Concord. Chemnitz and Chytraeus (a professor at the University of Rostock in northern Germany) revised the document, which now became known as the Swabian-Saxon Concord.

The discovery of Calvinists posing as Lutherans at the University of Wittenberg (a story which will be told on pages 146—148) precipitated a more determined search for a solution to the problems annoying the Lutherans. Elector August, who discovered the plot, urged the writing of a document called the Maulbronn Formula and then took the lead in assembling theologians from various territories at Torgau in 1576. These theologians, using the Swabian-Saxon Concord as a base with material from the Maulbronn Formula, produced the Torgau Book. This was then circulated among the Lutheran territories for opinions. Generally the replies were favorable. Andreae, Chemnitz, and Chytraeus worked through it again, reviewing the suggestions that had been made. The Torgau Book reedited by these three theologians and reviewed by others became known as the Bergen Book. This document became the Solid Declaration (or Thorough Declaration) of the Formula of Concord. It was finished in 1577 and is placed last among the historic Lutheran Confessions.

The Bergen Book or the Solid Declaration was criticized by some for what was considered its excessive length. We can appreciate this kind of criticism about many writings; they are just too long and complex. To answer these criticisms, Andreae prepared a synopsis or abridgement called the Epitome of the Formula of Concord. The Epitome presents the same material, article for article, as does the Solid Declaration, but in shorter form. It can be scanned quickly to learn the controverted points and the Lutheran answer to them. For a deeper theological explanation the Solid Declaration can be consulted. Together the Solid Declaration and the Epitome make up the Formula of Concord.

The support throughout Germany given to the Formula of Concord was overwhelming. A total of 8,188 Lutheran pastors and theologians along with 51 governmental leaders signed it. It was called the Formula of Concord because it restored peace and harmony among the Lutherans through doctrinal agreement. A badly fractured Lutheranism was healed.

To celebrate the restoration of doctrinal concord, the publication of all the Lutheran Confessions was scheduled for June 25, 1580, the 50th anniversary of the presentation of the Augsburg Confession. The volume containing the Lutheran Confessions was called the *Book of Concord.* Its contents are listed on pages 16—17. The fact that (since he was long dead) Luther did not participate in the preparation and writing of the Formula of Concord or the gathering of the Lutheran Confessions in the *Book of Concord* shows the great doctrinal and confessional strength of Lutheranism. It does not revolve around the personality of one man or devotion to him.

The Latin word for the *Book of Concord* is "Concordia," and it is used as an abbreviation for the collection of Lutheran Confessions very much in the sense that "Augustana" is used as the abbreviation for the Augsburg Confession. "Concordia" is still in popular use among Lutherans, especially as a name for colleges, seminaries, and churches. Wherever it is used, it should remind us of our allegiance to the Confessions.

The Formula of Concord in both the Solid Declaration and the Epitome has 12 articles. The order of these articles in the Formula does not suggest the time sequence in which the problems they address appeared. Each of the 12 articles has the same organizational structure. First there is a reference to the historical problem in the church, but without mentioning the names of the men involved. Second, the correct

Lutheran answer is given. Finally, the objectionable points in the opponents' position are listed. This clear-cut method of organization makes each article easy to understand as a self-contained unit. A brief discussion of each article is given here.

Article I

The first article, "Original Sin," handles one of those problems which should never have arisen, because those involved appear to have gotten caught in their own words. Lutherans have held a very firm position on original sin. In their previous confessional writings they had heavily scored the Roman Catholics for holding that unconverted man could contribute to his salvation. This doctrine is also called synergism. Unfortunately, certain Lutherans, including Melanchthon, began to lean in this direction after Luther's death. Central to Luther's doctrine of justification by grace through faith alone, however, is the concomitant doctrine that man does not and cannot contribute anything to his salvation. Luther came to this opinion through his study of the Scriptures and through bitter personal experience. One of Luther's most ardent supporters, Matthias Flacius, in his zeal to present Luther's position had taken original sin to an extreme by asserting that human nature itself is sin. The Lutheran position is that human nature is sinful but that it can hardly be equated with sin. The logical conclusion of Flacius' assertion would make God the cause of sin, since He created human nature. The Formula rejects this erroneous view by asserting that human nature itself is not sin because God created it, the Son of God assumed it in the Incarnation, and God will resurrect it on the last day. Lutherans insist, however, that sin lives in every corner of human nature.

Article II

The second article, "Free Will," speaks to the error of synergism, the position that unconverted man makes a contribution to his salvation. Melanchthon had written that the three causes of man's salvation were the Spirit, the Word, and the nonresisting will of man. The last cause was attacked as synergistic, as it attributed something good to unconverted man in the process of salvation. The issue of cooperation was not addressed to man as he was first created in holiness, or in regeneration, or in the final glorification. In these three instances man's will is already under divine influence. The Philippists were asserting that in a state of sin man could cooperate in coming to salvation.

The Formula of Concord puts forth as the Lutheran view Martin Luther's position in his famous Reformation writing *The Bondage of the Will.* Luther had directed this work against Erasmus' *Freedom of the Will* early in the Reformation. Erasmus was a famous Dutch humanist, responsible for editing the Greek New Testament from which Luther had made his German translation. The humanist tradition, born and bred in the Renaissance, attributed to human nature lofty possibilities. In the Lutheran view man in his natural state is not only blind and deaf to God's working but becomes God's enemy. Left to his own devices he resists and struggles against God at every opportunity.

God does not force a person to believe against his will, but the Spirit working through the Word kindles faith. To this process man contributes nothing. Man's total inability to respond to God by his own power is the necessary backdrop for Lutheran doctrine. As long as man is regarded as contributing in any way to his salvation, he might be saved by grace, but not by grace *alone.*

Article III

"The Righteousness of Faith Before God," the subject of the third article, handles a problem that seems to be without exact parallel in church history. Twin errors are dealt with. Andreas Osiander, a Lutheran theologian, had taught that justification occurs with the indwelling of Christ's divine nature in man. Francesco Stancaro, an Italian professor at Koenigsberg, Germany, defended the opposite side of the coin by contending that justification occurs with the indwelling of Christ's human nature.

The Formula sees some very serious ramifications in these rarely held views. Both hold to an intolerable separation of the two natures of Christ. Even more serious were Osiander and Stancaro's mutually held definition of justification as the indwelling of Christ in the believer. This view is soundly rejected by the Formula. It sees justification as a judicial act of God through which He declares the sinner righteous on account of Christ by faith. Justification is not a *something* which happens *in* man, as they taught. Occurring in man is sanctification, a necessary concomitant and result of justification, but in no way to be equated or confused with it. If justification did happen within man, he would look to himself instead of to Christ for salvation. Lutherans certainly hold to the indwelling of Christ in Christians, but this indwelling is the result of justification, not its cause. By putting justification within man instead of seeing it as an act before God, Osiander and Stancaro were in fact reverting to the Roman Catholic view of justification as an ongoing process coming to completion in the Christian's life.

Article IV

The Lutherans' doctrine that justification does not depend on good works immediately brought upon them the charge that they were opposed to doing good works. Article XX of the Augsburg Confession, the longest of the doctrinal articles, shows the Lutheran sensitivity to this undeserved accusation. Article IV in the Formula, "Good Works," takes up the issue again. The Leipzig Interim referred to good works as being necessary for salvation. Some Lutheran theologians found these terms of the Interim acceptable and favorably quoted certain phrases from Melanchthon's writings to support their view. George Major stated this erroneous position without hesitation. He said that good works are necessary for salvation and that without good works no one can be saved. Nicholas von Amsdorf reacted to this and fell into the opposite trap of stating that good works are detrimental to salvation. Depending on the situations in which these phrases are spoken, both could be wrong or both could be correct. The Formula answers: Good works are necessary, but the phrase "for salvation" should be omitted. Faith does not have the option of refusing to perform good works. The Christian performs them without coercion. But in the question of salvation, of justification before God, good works have no role to play.

Article V

The Gospel as the good news that God has provided salvation for all men for Christ's sake is central in Lutheran theology. For some Lutherans, however, the Gospel's centrality was interpreted to mean that it was the only valid Word of God for them. Those who were so Gospel-oriented were regretfully led to accept the false opinion that the Law plays no part in the life of the Christian. Article V, "Law and Gospel," discusses the function of Law and Gospel and their relationship to each other. Those who held anti-Law views were called "antinomians," a word taken over from the Greek, meaning those who are opposed to the Law.

The problem of antinomianism had arisen already during Luther's lifetime. The reformer had to deal with a certain John Agricola's teaching that the Gospel and not the Law has the power to effect repentance in the sinner. Agricola's views, confusing the Law and the Gospel, had little influence. After Luther's death, however, the problem of the role of the Law in the life of the Christian broke out again in other forms.

The Formula of Concord recognizes that the term "Gospel" can be used in several ways and acknowledges that the Scriptures themselves have a variety of uses for the word. But when "Gospel" is used in the phrase "Law and Gospel," it refers to the preaching of salvation in Christ. The functions of the Law can in no way be transferred to the Gospel. Both the Law and the Gospel must be preached. The Law with its threats work repentance, and the Gospel as the proclamation of Christ's work effects faith. Without the Law, the Gospel cannot be comprehended; without the Gospel, the Law either drives men to despair or makes them hypocrites.

Christ's crucifixion is an example of how one historical event can be used to preach both Law and Gospel. His death shows how severe was the penalty of our sin. This would be an example of Law preaching, because we become fully aware of the seriousness of our sin. But when the crucifixion is preached to show that sins are no longer counted against us, then the Gospel is being preached. Historical events are in themselves neither Law nor Gospel, but they can be preached so that they become either Law or Gospel. Therefore Law and Gospel are categories through which the entire Biblical account is to be focused so that people may first acknowledge and repent of their sins and then believe that they have a gracious God in Christ Jesus.

Article VI

Article VI of the Formula of Concord, "The Third Function of the Law," is a continuation of the previous one, "Law and Gospel." It speaks of the validity and usefulness of the Law in the Christian life. Most Lutherans will remember from their catechism instruction that the Law has three uses— curb, mirror, and rule. This threefold distinction is set forth in Article VI and is thoroughly Lutheran.

The Law as a curb is applied by government to curb outward forms of evil and to maintain good order. Luther saw the Law functioning through the government as an extension of God the Creator. This first use of the Law became part of Luther's explanation ("good government") of "Give us this day our daily bread" in the Lord's Prayer.

The second use refers to the Law as a mirror where man sees his sin and is brought to repentance. This subject is discussed in Article V, "Law and Gospel."

The third use, addressed in Article VI, concerns the validity of the Law in the Christian's life. While some acknowledged the other two uses, they failed to see the Law's application in the life of the Christian. They held that it was meant for evil men but not for those who had become free in the Gospel. The Formula of Concord asserts that the Law which condemns the unregenerate person assumes a new appearance in the regenerate life of a Christian. It now informs the Christian about what pleases God. Only the Gospel can be the motive for good works, but the Law educates the Christian about what form those works are to take. Luther himself had provided concrete examples of the teaching, or didactic, use of the Law in his explanations of the Ten Commandments.

Article VII

Many points have traditionally divided Lutheranism from the Reformed theology associated with Ulrich Zwingli and John Calvin, but the most divisive point has been the Lord's Supper. Concepts about it among the Reformed were expressed differently, but they agreed in opposing the Lutheran position on the bread and wine being Christ's body and blood. The differences between the two groups were already articulated when Luther met with Zwingli at Marburg in October 1529. Article VII, "The Holy Supper," is the Lutheran answer to Reformed ideas that had been adopted in some Lutheran circles.

Philip Melanchthon is considered responsible for funneling into the Lutheran Church Reformed or Calvinistic views on the Lord's Supper. Melanchthon's 1540 edition of the Augsburg Confession, known as the "Variata," permitted Calvin's spiritualizing concept.

Calvinists now found it possible to spread their views using phrases that were generally associated with

Lutheranism. Remember that false doctrine is nearly always guilty of using deceptive language. The use of Lutheran phrases to propagate Calvin's teachings was called "Crypto-Calvinism," which means Calvinism hidden under another guise, in this case Lutheranism.

The center of this Crypto-Calvinistic heresy was the University of Wittenberg, the historic birthplace of the Lutheran Reformation. Important in this situation was Elector August of Saxony, the successor of his brother Maurice as head of electoral Saxony. Alerted by many theologians and others, August suspected that something was amiss on the theological faculty at Wittenberg and began to make inquiries. He addressed direct and pertinent questions to the professors. Their replies consisted of quotations from Luther, generally accompanied with ambiguous ones from Melanchthon, coupled with attacks on Flacius and others who had been accusing them. So effective was the propaganda of the Crypto-Calvinists that Elector August began removing the remaining true Lutherans from the Wittenberg faculty. Then, suddenly, August's eyes were opened.

A letter was delivered to the wrong person. Written by Casper Peucer, Melanchthon's son-in-law and a member of the Crypto-Calvinistic conspiracy at Wittenberg, it was intended for a like-minded court preacher, urging him to influence the elector's wife by giving her a Calvinistic prayer book. By mistake the letter was delivered to an orthodox court preacher, who showed it to the elector. The conspiracy had been discovered! After subsequent investigations the faculty was dismissed and genuinely Lutheran professors were brought in.

What the Formula of Concord had to say about the Lord's Supper became all the more meaningful and crucial because of this experience at Wittenberg. Article VII is written directly against this backdrop.

In Article VII Luther's writings and the other confessional documents are generously quoted. The Lutherans see the Lord's Supper as a union between the earthly elements of bread and wine and Christ's body and blood. This is called the sacramental union. The strongest attacks are reserved for the "Sacramentarian" (Reformed) views denying the Real Presence. Sixteen different views are condemned. Four arguments from Luther's *Confession Concerning the Lord's*

Supper of 1528 are taken over into the Formula: 1. Jesus is inseparably God and man. 2. Jesus is at God's right hand and is therefore everywhere and capable of doing all things. 3. The Word of God does not lie. 4. God is not limited to one place at a time.

Article VIII

When Lutherans defended the Real Presence against the Reformed it became evident that there were serious differences between the two groups in regard to Christology (the doctrine of Christ). The Formula of Concord's Article VIII, "The Person of Christ," was directed to these important questions.

Differences between Lutheran and Reformed Christology surfaced in the very first talks on the Lord's Supper between Luther and Zwingli. Luther took exception to Zwingli's view that the human body of Christ was so confined to God's right hand that it could in no way be present on earth in the Lord's Supper. For Luther God's right hand was wherever God demonstrated His power. Zwingli saw God's right hand as an actual place where Christ's human nature but not His divine nature was confined. Calvin did not advance beyond Zwingli's view in this matter. Reformed theologians and those whom they have influenced in Lutheranism still operate with this idea.

For the Reformed the divine and human natures in Christ are so distinct that they operate alongside one another, not through one another as taught in Lutheranism. The Reformed would not attribute to Jesus' human nature divine attributes, qualities, and worship. A human nature which remains untouched and uninfused by the divine nature cannot possibly be present on earth wherever the Lord's Supper is celebrated.

The Lutherans saw the Reformed position as a revival of the ancient heresy of Nestorianism which held that Christ's two natures exist side by side in a mutually nonparticipating relationship. For the Lutherans Calvinistic thinking came close to a denial of the personal union within Christ. Led to its natural conclusion, Nestorianism in any form leads to asserting that two personalities are found in Jesus and to a denial of a real incarnation.

Article VIII reaffirms the decisions of the Council of Chalcedon in A.D. 451. This council rejected Nestorianism and affirmed the mutual interpenetration of Christ's two natures and their attitudes. Article VIII confesses that the Son of God became man and that through this action there was a union between the divine and human natures in such a way that one nature is always present with the other and each participates in all actions of the other. For a better understanding of Christ's Person the Lutherans developed three categories to describe but not explain this mysterious union.

The first category describes Christ as only one Person who has divine and human qualities, but the divine qualities are assigned to the divine nature and the human qualities to the human nature. The second category states that Christ performs both human and divine acts, but the human nature is responsible for human acts and likewise the divine nature for divine acts. The third category was the most crucial. According to it, all of the attributes of Christ's divine nature are assigned to the human nature. (The human attributes are not assigned to the divine nature, however.) This happened in such a way that the human nature was not made equal with the divine nature and did not lose any of its humanity. With such a doctrine of the divine infusion into the human nature, the Lutherans had no difficulty asserting the presence of the human nature everywhere, including in the Lord's Supper. Christ's human nature is no more confined and imprisoned in one place than is God.

In such an understanding of the Person of Christ, the Lutherans were not merely hunting for ideological support for their understanding of Christ's presence in the Lord's Supper. Their view of Christ was a statement of their faith in the Incarnation. On this understanding of the Person of Christ and the Incarnation rested the doctrine of the Atonement—possible only because, as God, Jesus' sacrificial death had infinite worth. Without a total participation of the divine nature in the human nature, the death of Jesus would have no more value that than of a great martyr. This universal atonement, basing its value on the God-man Jesus Christ who offered Himself up, provided God with the basis for justifying believers on account of Christ. Lutheran doctrine is Christocentric throughout, and therefore it is absolutely essential that the correct doctrine about the Person of Christ be maintained.

In presenting their understanding of Christ's Person, the Lutherans made ample use of the Holy Scriptures and

Luther's writings. Still, their position was not new or peculiar to them but a restatement of the understanding of the ancient and catholic church. Again the Lutherans were demonstrating that they were no sect. Martin Chemnitz wrote a large book called *The Two Natures in Christ* (English translation by J. A. O. Preus put out by Concordia Publishing House, 1971) to show that the Lutheran position had the backing of the ancient church.

Article IX

The subject of Article IX of the Formula is "Christ's Descent into Hell." In the ancient church there had been no unanimous opinion about the meaning of the phrase in the Apostles' Creed "He descended into hell." Some thought it meant that after His death Christ released the Old Testament saints out of a special place reserved for them so that they could now enter heaven. A very popular view was Christ's victorious proclamation of His conquest of Satan. As the matter remained unsettled through centuries of church history, it is not surprising that a difference of opinion would arise among Lutheran theologians. A church official in Hamburg asserted that Christ's body remained in the grave, but His soul descended into hell as part of His humiliation and work of atonement for sins. Opponents of this view pointed to the words from the cross "It is finished!" as indicating Christ's completion of the work of atonement. This, the shortest of all articles in the Formula, puts forth its argument in four points: 1. Christ as God and man descended into hell. 2. This descent was a triumphal act of glorification and not part of His humiliation. 3. This article is to be accepted by faith without speculation about the details. 4. This doctrine grants comfort to Christians as it promises them victory over Satan and hell.

Some Lutherans today have entertained views about Christ's descent into hell which are directly contrary to this article. In some recent translations of the Apostles Creed His descent is explained merely as His dying. Such a view is not in agreement with Article IX of the Formula.

Article X

Article X of the Formula of Concord has the rather long title "The Ecclesiastical Rites That Are Called Adiaphora or Things Indifferent." Adiaphora is a Greek word that means "things morally indifferent" or "nonessentials in faith or conduct." It would hardly seem that the church would need an article of doctrine on things that really do not matter. But it was a controversy over adiaphora that precipitated the first recognizable split in Lutheran ranks after Luther's death.

The story of the emperor's success in subjugating Lutheran lands and forcing the Interims upon the people has been told at the beginning of this chapter. The Lutheran response to this was not unanimous. Philip Melanchthon supported the arrangement with the defense that it was the best the Lutherans could do in their state of subjugation. Matthias Flacius was sharply opposed to accepting the Interim. The answer given by Article X was the one adopted by Flacius, who refused to tolerate the reintroduction of Roman Catholic customs. Christians have freedom to practice or to avoid customs and rituals which are neither forbidden nor commanded in God's Word, but they are duty bound to resist where compliance in customs would give the impression that they were complying with false doctrine. Should a human ordinance be given the stature of a divine command or be viewed as necessary for salvation, it must be resisted.

The Lutherans at the time of the Reformation were not the first to encounter this kind of problem. In apostolic days circumcision had become an adiaphoron for Christians. While Paul agreed to the voluntary circumcision of Timothy in order to avoid offense, he refused to acquiesce to the demand of the Judaizers to circumcise Titus. Such compliance would have indicated that Paul agreed with the Judaizers' claim that circumcision was necessary for salvation.

Unlike many other denominational families, Lutherans do not have required customs or universally observed rites. Yet history shows that they are concerned with good order. From the very beginning Luther and his coreformers established worship regulations for the newly emerging Protestant churches. Some of these would seem strange to us now. The message of Article X is that no human ordinance can be insisted upon as being of divine right and that no custom which suggests submission to false doctrine can be tolerated.

Article XI

The subject of Article XI of the Formula, "God's Eternal

Foreknowledge and Divine Election," presents an issue that had not yet been a real problem amomg the Lutherans. The chief purpose for its inclusion was the prevention of future difficulties. Martin Luther had set forth the concept of God's grace in such an absolute way, without any allowance for man's participation in salvation, that it might be natural to assert that God is also the cause of man's damnation. This was never Luther's teaching. John Calvin and the Reformed, however, taught "double predestination": Some are predestined for heaven and others for hell.

Article XI first distinguishes between God's foreknowledge and election. By His foreknowledge God knows and comprehends all things good and evil before they happen, but He is in no way the cause of evil. This is distinct from Calvinism, where God is the ultimate cause of man's damnation. Lutherans do, however, teach that God is the sole cause and source of man's salvation. There is a deep mystery involved here as to why some are saved and others not, but Scripture teaches us not to speculate about such matters.

Faith is the Christian's evidence of his election. Election should not, however, be viewed as God's prior approval in eternity of man's faith. God does not choose man on account of faith. Just the opposite is the case. Faith is the result of election. The doctrine of election is only a restatement of the doctrine of grace as viewed by God in eternity.

God's purpose in revealing the doctrine of election is so that Christians may have comfort in the certainty of their salvation. On that account it is to be proclaimed to Christians, especially those who may be doubting their salvation.

Once could almost ascribe to the authors of the Formula of Concord the gift of prophecy for their foresight in including this article about divine election. About 300 years later a controversy over this issue broke out among Lutherans in the United States, fracturing the confessional unity which conservative Lutherans had worked for. Differences on this issue among Lutherans in the last part of the 1800s are still regarded as a major cause for the different Lutheran groups today. In that controversy the answers provided by Article XI on predestination served a useful purpose.

Article XII

The first 11 articles of the Formula of Concord are

addressed to problems among the Lutheran theologians themselves. The 12th and final article speaks not of problems among Lutherans but of other religious groups. It is entitled "Other Factions and Sects Which Never Accepted the Augsburg Confession." Mentioned by name are the Anabaptists, the Schwenkfelders, the New Arians, and the New Anti-Trinitarians. From the very beginning the Lutherans opposed these and similar movements. It may be speculated that Luther's Reformation uncorked many underground feelings, but he and his followers never approved of such groups. A conglomeration of unacceptable views are gathered for rejection in this article. Among them are: Jesus was not God, but only a highly endowed man; only adults and not children should be baptized; participation in government is wrong; the sacraments do not offer grace. Most of these views are still held by many religious groups today. Sad to say, some Lutherans also hold similar opinions.

Epilog

By 1580 the age of the Reformation was coming to a close and the church was embarking on another period. As much as the church would like to stand still, history propels it along.

The 1600s were a time of theological amplification. That century witnessed much theological industry, which produced the great classical dogmatical works of Lutheranism. However, that century also saw the Roman Catholic Counter-Reformation bring large areas of Europe back under the papacy, and it was the time of the Thirty Years' War, which devastated Germany.

The church on earth—the "church militant"—can never expect to reach a plateau of theological peace. This goal is reserved for heaven. According to Jesus' parable of the sower, Satan constantly sows tares among the wheat. Late in the 1600s a movement called Pietism emerged. It stressed a religion of the heart and feelings. Falling into disrepute was a stricter confessional and orthodox Lutheranism. It was labeled a religion of the head. Under the influence of Pietism differences between Lutheranism and Calvinism no longer seemed insurmountable.

More drastic than Pietism were the effects of Rationalism and the Enlightenment in the 1700s. European Christianity and not only Lutheranism was brought to near extinction by the end of that century. Many countries remained officially Lutheran in name, but the confessional Lutheranism of the 1500s was no longer a living reality. The people were taught that the mind and not the Bible alone was the source of religious truth—men did not really need Christian revelation to know about God; they could use nature and their minds. Even our century, which is scored for its materialism, never hit the dregs of that time. But a miracle in the early 1800s, comparable to Luther's discovery of justification in the

1500s, brought a reawakening and a new awareness of confessional truth.

A number of theologians, most of them young theological students, began reading Luther, the Lutheran Confessions, and Lutheran theologians again and discovered that Luther's faith was not being taught at Lutheran universities and was not being preached from Lutheran pulpits. Many Germans and Scandinavians caught up in this confessional awakening emigrated to the United States in the mid 1800s with the express purpose of preserving confessional Lutheranism. The Lutheran Church—Missouri Synod is a direct result of this awakened confessional interest. Most other Lutheran synods in the United States have roots leading back to the same movement.

Each Lutheran congregation and synod as it has come into existence has obligated itself in its constitution to accepting the Lutheran Confessions. Not all Lutheran groups have accepted the entire *Book of Concord*. Some have accepted only the Augsburg Confession and the Small Catechism. Some Scandinavian churches do not see the Formula of Concord as part of their heritage and do not feel the same commitment to it as do the German churches. Some Lutheran churches have confessional statements in addition to those in the *Book of Concord*. Various Lutheran groups have at various times had to respond to their particular problems with confessional statements. True confessional Lutheranism involves not only a formal allegiance to the historic faith of the church; it also means that that faith is actually preached and taught. In such churches the true spirit of the Lutheran confessors is still alive.

When the Lutheran theologians prepared the *Book of Concord* and subscribed their signatures in 1580, they were not writing "E-N-D" to the preparation of any more confessions. This would be the last thing in the mind of any confessor. The story of the Lutheran Confessions will not come to an end until Jesus returns in glory. For historic confessions to become living statements of the truth, they must be reexpressed by each generation. No generation can guarantee the confessional quality of future ones. Preparations for the future can be made, but the future must make its own decisions. The light of confessional fervor can be snuffed out as easily as it can burst into a living flame. The church must be alert to the danger of confessionalism turning into mere historicism, interest in the past for its own sake without personal commitment. The Confessions must be studied as statements of our own faith and not just as relics from our past. Where they are no longer studied there is little chance that the faith they profess will be maintained.

Our Confessions arose in a variety of circumstances. Though the problems the church faced in the 1500s had been troublesome in previous centuries, the documents coming from that century were by God's providence given permanent confessional status. Many who read the signs of the times believe that the church is now ready for another confessional awakening. While some of the problems faced 400 years ago remain the same, new ones have arisen. One faced not only by Lutherans but by Christians in nearly all denominations is the false assertion that the Biblical accounts do not report historical occurrences. Such views hold that we can have no certainty about the events reported in the Bible. This problem seems to be no less crucial than the heresy encountered in the fourth century that denied Christ's eternal deity or in the 16th century that denied man's justification before God through faith alone. There is no rule about the length of time a problem has to plague the church before it responds in confession. In the case of the Arian heresy, the response of the Council of Nicaea was almost instantaneous. The problems resulting in the historic Lutheran Confessions were with the church for over a thousand years before the church adequately handled them. The problem which denies the history reported in the Bible or which considers it insignificant deserves a definitive confessional answer. Our generation will write its own history about her strength to provide such an answer. After this problem disappears, the church will be plagued by new ones. In each case the church is under obligation from her Lord to respond.

On this account the story of the Lutheran Confessions is never over. The *Book of Concord* is only a step, but a very important step, in a process that never comes to an end while time lasts.

Questions

I. HONORING A BOOK

1. How many organizations with which you are acquainted commemorate the *Book of Concord* by being designated "Concordia"?
2. How many denominations are represented in the churches of your community? Have you ever asked a member of one of these churches what the doctrines of that church are? Do they make any reference to their confessions or use them?
3. Look at your church constitution. List the names of the Lutheran Confessions found in the constitution of your congregation.
4. Ask the pastor for the *Agenda*. What Lutheran Confessions are found in the order of service admitting new members into your church?
5. Find the order of service for an ordination service and look for the place where the pastor makes his confessional subscription. Which Confessions are listed in this service?
6. What can be done in your church to make the members more aware of what it means to be "confessional"?
7. Are new members in our churches aware of the Lutheran Confessions? Can anything be done in confirmation instruction to stress their importance?

II. HOW IT ALL STARTED—THE BIBLICAL ORIGINS

1. In your own words give a definition of a confession.
2. How many groups to which you belong have entrance or membership requirements? How are these requirements different and similar to the requirements made for church membership in the Confessions?
3. Study Rom. 10:9-10. What did St. Paul see as necessary for the sinner's justification and salvation?
4. The Ten Commandments are at the heart of the Old Testament. What events surrounded their being given? Read Deut. 5.
5. Deut. 6:4 contains the great confession of Israel. What were the other requirements associated with this great confession? Read verses 1-9 in this chapter.
6. Matt. 16:16 contains the great confession of Jesus as the Christ. Others thought that Jesus was not the Christ. According to verses 13 and 14, who did they think Jesus was?
7. From your own knowledge of the Old Testament list certain characteristics of the Christ, the promised Deliverer.
8. Read Phil. 2:5-11 and find the similarities between this passage and the Apostles' Creed. Categorize the statements according to either humiliation or exaltation.
9. Find those sections of our worship service where the Trinity is mentioned.
10. In which situations are Christians most easily tempted to deny Christ? How should Christians encourage one another so that they confess Jesus instead of denying Him?

III. THE CATHOLIC TRADITION

1. The word "catholic" has many meanings. From your own experience give several of these meanings.
2. What does Jesus mean by the words "spirit" and "flesh" when they appear together? What did Greek philosophy mean by these same terms? When the apostle St. John wrote that "the Word became flesh," what did he mean by "flesh"?
3. The Apostles' Creed combats heresies that thought Jesus' humanity was unimportant, while the Nicene Creed opposes heresies that denied His deity. Find parallels in the present time to these ancient problems.
4. In what sense is the world both good and evil?
5. What is the significance of the word "only" and of the phrase "under Pontius Pilate" in the Apostles' Creed?
6. Luther recited the Apostles' Creed several times a day. What can be done to encourage a more frequent use of this creed in the private and corporate worship of the members of the congregation?
7. Which countries have vestiges of "Constantinian Christianity"? What are the advantages and disadvantages of a state-related or -controlled Christianity?
8. Do you think Lutherans should be more informed about the Holy Trinity? How does our church compare with others in the attention it gives this central doctrine of Christianity?
9. List those phrases in the Nicene Creed in which the deity of Jesus is affirmed. What is the distinct contribution of each of these phrases in asserting His deity?
10. Read through the Athanasian Creed, on page 53 of *The Lutheran Hymnal*. Find the divisions in this creed where it speaks about the Trinity and about Jesus. Make two lists. On one list put down what is confessed about the Trinity and on the other what is confessed about Christ.

IV. CONFESSIONAL AWAKENING AT AUGSBURG

1. The year 1980 is the 450th anniversary of the presentation of the Augsburg Confession. Suggest to the pastor the possibility of reading one of the 21 doctrinal articles each Sunday as part of the church service.
2. Arrange study groups in the congregation to read the Augsburg Confession and to discuss it.
3. The Augsburg Confession was presented by princes to the emperor. List as many ways as possible in which Christians today present their confessions. What confessional avenues are open to Christians living under Communist domination?
4. How are the doctrines of Holy Scripture and justification by faith related in Lutheran theology?
5. It has been 450 years since the Augsburg Confession was presented to Roman Catholic officials. In which ways has the Roman Catholic Church changed? In which ways has it remained the same?
6. How do Lutheran views of man as a totally depraved sinner compare with modern views?
7. Let individual members in the group each list one Lutheran doctrine—for example, Baptism, The Christian Life, etc. Together discuss how that doctrine centers around Christ.
8. If any members have traveled in the Lutheran countries of Europe, let them compare Lutheranism there with that in North America. How do others feel about the church receiving contributions from the government?

V. THE APOLOGY—THE MELANCHTHONIAN STORM

1. Lutherans consider justification the chief article of the Christian religion. Let each member define it as he best knows how. Then let the pastor or other group leader compare the group's opinion with the Apology of the Augsburg Confession.
2. How do Lutherans and Roman Catholics differ on the concept of good works? What role do good works play in Lutheranism? in Roman Catholicism?
3. What is "work-righteousness"? How are Christians constantly confronted with this danger?
4. How does Melanchthon's tone in the Apology differ from that in the Augsburg Confession? How do you account for this difference?

VI. SMALCALD—GETTING READY FOR THE BATTLE NEVER FOUGHT

1. Determine how Protestant church leaders feel about the pope today. Can you list any leaders who have visited him?
2. Many Roman Catholics, including some bishops and priests, publicly differ with the pope. Can you list any areas of differences where they have criticized him?
3. List ways in which the pope continues to exercise authority in the church. Has he relinquished any of his claims?
4. Any reunion or accommodation between Protestants and Roman Catholics will have to discuss the question of papal supremacy in the church. Discuss the right of any one man to rule absolutely in the church.
5. In your opinion does Luther's verdict of "Antichrist" still apply to the pope? Could it possibly apply also to others besides him?

VII. OTHER BUSINESS AT SMALCALD—MELANCHTHON'S TREATISE ON THE POWER AND PRIMACY OF THE POPE

1. Discuss the leadership and governing procedures in your church.
2. What are the responsibilities of the local congregation, the District, and the Synod to one another?
3. Different Lutheran groups (don't forget those overseas) have different governing procedures. Describe these and discuss them. What do you see as the advantages and disadvantages of each?

VIII. THE PASTORAL HEART—LUTHER'S TWO CATECHISMS

1. How many members in the group can remember any of the sections of Luther's Small Catechism which they may have committed to memory at the time of their confirmation?
2. Luther's Small Catechism as given in the *Book of Concord* is somewhat longer than the one generally learned by the children. Ask the pastor for his copy of the *Book of Concord* and have a member read the sections that are unfamiliar. Also ask the pastor for some information about the large number of questions and answers (not from Luther) that make up the bulk of the catechisms generally used among Lutherans.
3. Discuss ways in which the congregation can commemorate the 450th anniversary of Luther's catechisms in 1979. Several possibilities include a series of sermons on each of the parts of the Small Catechism, reading one section of the Large Catechism as the sermon for one Sunday, or having the congregation for a number of Sundays recite together (after the creed) a section of Luther's Small Catechism.

IX. GETTING THE LOG OUT OF YOUR OWN EYE—THE FORMULA OF CONCORD

1. In what ways is man's nature evil? In which ways is it good? How do Lutheran views of man differ from those held in other denominations?
2. Frequently Christians are asked to make a "decision for Christ." Does this agree with the Lutheran view about free will?
3. Let each person define justification. Compare the views expressed with those of the Formula in Article III.
4. What does the Formula mean when it says that good works are necessary? In what way are good works unnecessary?
5. Choose several events from Christ's life and show how each can be used to preach the Law and the Gospel.
6. How is the Lutheran view of the Lord's Supper different from that of most other Protestants and that of the Roman Catholics?
7. How is it possible to confess such things as God died on the cross? Mary is the mother of God? Jesus of Nazareth fills heaven and earth with His glory?
8. The descent of Christ into hell signifies Christ's victory over Satan. What importance do you see in the rise of the occult, devotion to Satan, in our time?
9. How many different types of gowns have you seen Lutheran pastors wear during church services? Lutherans have no laws about these things. What are the dangers in individualism? in conformity? What would you consider acceptable and offensive in these matters?

EPILOG

1. Ask the pastor for a list of the confessional statements produced by your church body in recent years.
2. What are the central issues discussed in these documents?
3. Do you feel that there are some important issues to which your church should address itself confessionally?
4. Are there problems in the church today that would necessitate one or several large meetings?